LEARN MLFLOW

*Manage Machine Learning Pipelines
and Models Efficiently*

Diego Rodrigues

LEARN MLFLOW
Manage Machine Learning Pipelines and Models Efficiently

2025 Edition
Author: Diego Rodrigues
studiod21portoalegre@gmail.com

Published by StudioD21.

Important Note

The code and scripts presented in this book are primarily intended to practically illustrate the concepts discussed throughout the chapters. They were developed to demonstrate didactic applications in controlled environments and may therefore require adaptations to function correctly in different contexts. It is the reader's responsibility to validate the specific configurations of their development environment before practical implementation.

More than providing ready-made solutions, this book seeks to encourage a solid understanding of the covered fundamentals, promoting critical thinking and technical autonomy. The presented examples should be viewed as starting points for the reader to develop their own solutions—original and tailored to the real demands of their career or projects. True technical competence arises from the ability to internalize essential principles and apply them creatively, strategically, and transformatively.

We encourage every reader to go beyond merely replicating examples, using this content as a foundation to build their own code and scripts with unique identity, capable of making a significant impact on their professional journey. This is the spirit of applied knowledge: to learn deeply in order to innovate with purpose.

Thank you for your trust, and we wish you a productive and inspiring study journey.

CONTENTS

GREETINGS

It is with great enthusiasm that I welcome you to dive into the world of efficiency and total control over Machine Learning pipelines and models through MLflow. Your initiative to master this powerful platform demonstrates a clear commitment to professional growth and the pursuit of scalable and effective solutions for Data Science and Machine Learning projects.

In this book, LEARN MLflow – Manage Machine Learning Pipelines and Models Efficiently, you will find a structured and fully practice-oriented approach, aimed at professionals and enthusiasts who wish to go beyond the basics. Each chapter is designed to provide progressive knowledge, from essential environment setup to advanced strategies for integration and pipeline automation.

Your choice to invest time in MLflow reflects an awareness that success in Machine Learning is not limited to creating accurate algorithms, but also relies on efficient experiment management, consistent reproducibility, and reliable model deployment. Your mastery will offer a valuable edge, enabling the development of solutions focused on concrete, measurable, and continuously improvable results.

Throughout these chapters, you will access practical concepts, carefully crafted examples, and dedicated sections on common errors, best practices, and strategic summaries. This structure ensures not only conceptual understanding but also immediate application in professional settings, allowing each technique learned to be easily tested and integrated into real-world development scenarios.

Get ready to deepen your knowledge, tackle challenges, and achieve unmatched control over the entire lifecycle of Machine Learning models. It is a pleasure to have you on this journey toward excellence in AI project management, and I hope each topic covered becomes a powerful tool in building robust, scalable solutions aligned with the best market practices.

Welcome, and enjoy your reading!

ABOUT THE AUTHOR

Diego Rodrigues
Technical Author and Independent Researcher
ORCID: https://orcid.org/0009-0006-2178-634X
StudioD21 Smart Tech Content & Intell Systems
E-mail: studiod21portoalegre@gmail.com
LinkedIn: www.linkedin.com/in/diegoxpertai

International technical author (*tech writer*) focusing on structured production of applied knowledge. He is the founder of StudioD21 Smart Tech Content & Intell Systems, where he leads the creation of intelligent frameworks and the publication of technical textbooks supported by artificial intelligence, such as the Kali Linux Extreme series, SMARTBOOKS D21, among others.

Holder of 42 international certifications issued by institutions such as IBM, Google, Microsoft, AWS, Cisco, META, Ec-Council, Palo Alto and Boston University, he works in the fields of Artificial Intelligence, Machine Learning, Data Science, Big Data, Blockchain, Connectivity Technologies, Ethical Hacking and Threat Intelligence.

Since 2003, he has developed more than 200 technical projects for brands in Brazil, USA and Mexico. In 2024, he established himself as one of the greatest authors of technical books of the new generation, with more than 180 titles published in six languages. His work is based on his own applied technical writing protocol TECHWRITE 2.2, aimed at scalability, conceptual precision and practical applicability in professional environments.

BOOK PRESENTATION

In this book, *LEARN MLflow – Manage Machine Learning Pipelines and Models Efficiently*, we have gathered the most important content to enable you to orchestrate the entire lifecycle of your Machine Learning projects in an organized, scalable, and secure way. We begin with a fundamental overview of what MLflow is and why it has become an indispensable tool for Data Science professionals seeking reproducibility and version control in their experiments. Next, we explore model management and the underlying architecture, clarifying how each component (Tracking, Projects, Models, and Model Registry) interacts to streamline everything from initial setup to the registration and monitoring of deployed models.

We then move on to the installation and environment configuration, guiding you on how to ensure everything works properly, even in scenarios where teamwork and resource sharing are essential parts of the project. Following that, we dive into the practical use of MLflow for logging parameters, metrics, and artifacts, demonstrating how this facilitates result comparison and the selection of the best approach. Gradually, we introduce the functionalities of MLflow Projects, Model Registry, CI/CD pipeline integration, and ways to visualize and analyze metrics, covering everything from classical tasks to feature engineering strategies and concerns about security and permissions.

From there, the focus shifts to more complex scenarios, such as artifact scaling, deployment on cloud providers, and model monitoring processes in production, emphasizing how to overcome infrastructure challenges and integrate into corporate environments. We also discuss real-world examples of MLflow usage in large companies, reinforcing the practical relevance of the concepts throughout the content. Specific chapters are dedicated to integrations with AutoML, Spark, Big Data, and hyperparameter optimization methodologies, showing how to manage robust workflows and fully leverage the platform.

The final chapters bring together consolidated best practices, failure cases, and contingency plans, along with a comprehensive checklist for MLflow projects, providing a unified view that consolidates all critical points discussed. Thus, this book offers a complete experience, allowing you, the reader, to not only gain technical mastery of MLflow's features but also the confidence to apply each step in real-world scenarios and extract reliable insights to evolve your Machine Learning solutions.

CHAPTER 1. OVERVIEW OF MLFLOW

The advancement of Machine Learning solutions in the corporate and academic sectors has significantly changed how models are developed, trained, and delivered. The creation of isolated models without systematic control over versions, hyperparameters, or generated artifacts quickly became a technical and operational problem. As project scale increased, specific needs for standardization, tracking, reproducibility, and reliable deployment emerged. It was in this context that MLflow established itself as one of the leading frameworks for managing the Machine Learning lifecycle, offering a modular, flexible platform that is independent of specific languages or frameworks.

Originating from Databricks, MLflow was created to fill a clear gap: the lack of a lightweight yet robust tool that unified experimentation processes, model versioning, and deployment management. Unlike closed platforms or those tightly coupled to a single stack, MLflow prioritizes interoperability and technical freedom. It allows engineering and data science teams to collaborate consistently without relying on ad hoc practices or manual scripts to track experiment progress.

The structure of MLflow is organized into four main components. Each addresses a specific issue within the operational flow of Machine Learning:

MLflow Tracking
This is the heart of experiment tracking. It allows you to log

runs, compare metrics, store parameters, and version artifacts. This layer is essential for answering questions like "What was the best model we trained for this problem?" or "What changed in this new version, and why did it perform differently?"

MLflow Projects

Defines a convention for the directory and file structure that facilitates experiment reproducibility. The idea is simple: encapsulate the environment and commands needed to run an ML project in a portable way, whether locally or on remote servers.

MLflow Models

Organizes and saves trained models in reusable formats, enabling them to be loaded, served as REST APIs, or even deployed to production servers with minimal intervention.

Model Registry

Acts as a versioned model catalog, with access control, stage transitions (such as staging, production, and archived), and collaborative comments. It enables the approval and governance workflows many companies require before deploying a model.

These modules can be used independently, but when combined, they create a complete Machine Learning management platform. Modularity is one of MLflow's greatest advantages: it's not necessary to adopt the entire platform to benefit from it. Teams with existing pipelines can introduce MLflow gradually, adding tracking and control layers as needed.

Moreover, MLflow is not dependent on a specific modeling framework. It supports projects written in Python, R, Java, and even others, as long as commands can be invoked from a command line or REST interface. This allows multidisciplinary teams to adopt MLflow without drastically changing their established workflows.

Another key differentiator is its infrastructure independence. MLflow can run in local environments, on-premises servers, or in the cloud. It can use local file systems, relational databases, or cloud services to store experiments, artifacts, and models. This flexibility makes it suitable for both academic projects and large-scale operations in multinational companies with strict compliance and scalability requirements.

MLflow's direct impact on a data science team's productivity becomes evident when trying to reproduce an old experiment. Without proper tracking, it's common for superior models to be forgotten due to a lack of documentation, or for new versions to underperform because previous configurations are unknown. With MLflow, it's possible to compare versions, evaluate past decisions, restore old artifacts, and even re-run entire pipelines using the same parameters, data, and library versions.

This complete traceability brings technical security and fosters collaborative work. A team can work in a distributed and asynchronous manner, with each member logging their runs and discoveries in a structured way. This avoids rework, improves communication across departments, and drastically reduces the time needed to validate hypotheses or promote models to production.

Another important aspect is the centralization of technical documentation. When logging an experiment with MLflow, input parameters, evaluation metrics, logs, artifacts (such as CSV files, images, trained models), and even source code associated with the run are saved. This living documentation is automatically updated and can be accessed via graphical interface, command line, or REST API, facilitating integration with other tools in the data and engineering stack.

Beyond manual use, MLflow can also be automated. CI/CD pipelines can be configured to log experiments, train models, and update the Model Registry whenever there are changes in the code repository. This allows software engineering best practices (such as automated testing, versioning, and code review) to be integrated into Machine Learning development processes.

In production scenarios, MLflow also simplifies deployment management. With it, a model can be deployed directly as a REST endpoint, ready to serve predictions. Or it can be exported in formats compatible with services like SageMaker, Azure ML, or internal platforms. This interoperability speeds up time-to-deploy and reduces technical risks related to migrations and integrations.

Another strategic aspect is governance. Organizations needing to ensure reproducibility, traceability, and auditing of their models will find MLflow a natural ally. The ability to version models with access control, log technical comments, and document the logic of each version allows compliance requirements to be met without excessive bureaucracy.

Using MLflow also promotes the adoption of sound technical practices. By making parameters, metrics, and artifacts explicit, it forces the team to reflect on the structure of their experiments and clearly document decisions. This technical discipline reduces the accumulation of "experimentation debt" — the collection of models no one remembers how they were generated or what data was used to train them.

Throughout this book, these and other concepts will be explored in depth. Each chapter will focus on an essential MLflow component or practice, with practical examples, detailed code explanations, best practices, and strategic reflections. The goal is for you, the reader, to be able to structure a complete and reliable pipeline, using MLflow as the foundation to accelerate experimentation, support better decisions, and ensure operational excellence in your Machine Learning projects.

More than just learning commands and features, the goal is for you to master the technical rationale behind using a platform like MLflow. This expanded understanding will allow you to adapt solutions to your needs, personalize workflows, and lead your team to a new level of maturity in model management.

The journey begins with this broad, contextual vision. From here, each next step will be a practical advance toward building professional, auditable, and scalable pipelines. Mastery of MLflow is not just a competitive advantage — it is, today, a requirement for any team seeking to deliver reliable models in real-world environments.

CHAPTER 2. MODEL MANAGEMENT FUNDAMENTALS

Building high-quality Machine Learning models requires more than just understanding algorithms or manipulating datasets. In real-world environments, the difference between a one-off experiment and a professional solution lies in the ability to manage the model lifecycle with clarity, traceability, and security. Model management is not a technical luxury—it is a prerequisite for ensuring reproducibility, continuous performance, and operational reliability. This chapter explores the foundational principles that support this practice and explains why it has become central to modern Machine Learning engineering.

When we talk about managing models, we are referring to the entire journey a model undergoes: from hypothesis design, training, evaluation, cross-validation, and deployment, to post-deployment monitoring and continuous versioning. This journey, often called the ML Lifecycle, must be rigorously recorded and controlled to ensure every decision is auditable, every version is reproducible, and every change is justified. Ignoring this process is the shortest path to accumulating "ghost models"—files that no one knows where they came from or how they were created.

Machine Learning models, unlike traditional code, are products generated through a statistical and empirical process. This means that small variations in data, execution order, or hyperparameters can significantly alter the results. Therefore, versioning the training code alone is not enough: it's necessary to capture the execution context, input data, parameters, resulting metrics, and final artifacts. Without this structure, there is no reliable way to compare results or evolve solutions based on transparent technical decisions.

Model management begins with experiment tracking. Each training attempt should be logged as a unique run, with named parameters, clear metrics, and well-defined artifacts. Tools like MLflow Tracking were created precisely for this purpose: to automatically or manually capture the essential elements of each experiment and store them in an organized, accessible, and auditable manner. Using this approach allows models to be compared not just by final accuracy, but also by broader technical and operational criteria such as runtime, computational complexity, and result robustness.

Another essential pillar of management is versioning. Every approved model should be saved in a standardized format with complete metadata and predictable loading logic. MLflow Models, for instance, allows a model to be packaged as a Python function that can be reused, exported, or served as an API. This standardization reduces friction between science and engineering, facilitating the transition between experimentation and production environments. Moreover, it allows the model to be deployed across different platforms such as containers, serverless environments, or managed services.

Versioning should also include stage control. Not every model is ready for production as soon as it hits a satisfactory metric. It's common to define a promotion flow with intermediate stages such as "Staging" and "Validation" before releasing a "Production" version. This logic, implemented by MLflow's Model Registry, ensures a clear validation and approval process for models, with access control, technical comments, and explicit transitions. This flow prevents accidental deployments, facilitates rollback, and promotes a culture of technical responsibility for deployed models.

Integration between experimentation and operations is another common challenge. Models trained by data scientists need to be operationalized by engineers. Without a central point of documentation and versioning, this process becomes ad hoc and error-prone. Model management acts as a bridge between these two areas, standardizing inputs and outputs, logging decisions, and creating a technical history that can be followed by any team member. This alignment is essential for multidisciplinary teams where different professionals contribute at various stages of the model's lifecycle.

Artifact control is also a fundamental part of management. Beyond the trained model itself, it's important to save the datasets used, preprocessing scripts, generated visualizations, and execution logs. Each element contributes to the understanding and reproducibility of the final result. Tools like MLflow allow these artifacts to be stored in an organized way, with direct links to each run, making later inspection and technical auditing easier. This living documentation becomes a valuable asset for the team, who can revisit old models, reuse pipeline components, or extract insights from past decisions.

Another critical point is reproducibility. A model is only trustworthy if it can be regenerated from scratch using the same data, parameters, and environment. This requires not only code and data versioning, but also control over the execution environment—such as libraries, dependency versions, and hardware configuration. Using files like requirements.txt, conda.yaml, or even container images helps ensure the environment is reproducible. MLflow Projects expands on this logic by encapsulating all project dependencies in a single file, allowing it to be executed identically on different machines.

Reproducibility is especially important in regulated environments such as finance, healthcare, or energy. In these contexts, any decision made by a model must be justifiable and traceable. Model management ensures the ability to reconstruct the system state at the moment a prediction was made, providing legal and technical assurance for all stakeholders. Even in companies outside of these sectors, the ability to review past algorithmic decisions becomes a competitive advantage— especially in long-term projects or those with strategic impact.

It's also important to note that model management includes planned deprecation. Not every model needs to be retained indefinitely. Some will be replaced, others archived due to low performance or changes in business context. Having a clear lifecycle policy—with criteria for promotion, expiration, and archiving—helps keep the environment clean and organized. MLflow's Model Registry supports this type of control, allowing models to move between stages, add tags, archive old versions, and document the reasons for each transition.

Model management also facilitates organizational learning. By maintaining a structured history of attempts, failures, successes, and adjustments, the team gains visibility into what works and what doesn't. This accumulated knowledge enables faster and more accurate decisions in future projects. Instead of repeating experiments or making the same mistakes, it's possible to consult the history, analyze results, and build solutions from a solid foundation. Technical versioning becomes a mechanism for collective memory and continuous improvement.

Common Errors and Solutions

Error: "Run not recorded in tracking server"
Probable Cause: The MLflow tracking function (mlflow.start_run()) was not called or was improperly closed.
Recommended Solution: Explicitly start and end each run using mlflow.start_run() and mlflow.end_run(), ensuring the context is active during the entire experiment.

Error: "Model overwritten without warning"
Probable Cause: Reusing model name without version control during save.
Recommended Solution: Always use the Model Registry with automatic versioning or include a version number in the manually saved model name.

Error: "Conda environment not reproducible"
Probable Cause: Manual changes to the environment after generating conda.yaml.
Recommended Solution: Regenerate conda.yaml after each relevant change or use immutable environments via Docker.

Error: "Model registered but not deployed"
Probable Cause: Model approved in the registry but no deployment process linked.
Recommended Solution: Integrate Model Registry stage transition with CI/CD scripts or deployment services to ensure automated or supervised deployment.

Best Practices

- Use descriptive names for experiments, runs, and models —preferably with a standardized structure. This facilitates filtering, search, and future automation.

- Maintain consistency in parameter logging. Define fixed names and use the same pattern across all experiments (e.g., learning_rate, batch_size, dropout_rate) to avoid metric dispersion.

- Always save models with their associated metadata: training date, dataset used, preprocessing pipeline, target metric, and responsible technician. This enables faster queries and automated documentation.

- Define objective criteria for model promotion in the registry. For example: only promote to production if accuracy is above X, F1 score above Y, and response time below Z. These criteria can be automated in the CI/CD pipeline.

- Store all relevant execution artifacts, including auxiliary scripts, logs, reports, and visualizations. Even unused items may be valuable for audits or future analyses.

- Use tags and descriptions for saved models. A model without a description is an abandoned model. A short phrase about the model's goal already helps contextualize its purpose.

- Automate the cleanup of old versions and obsolete runs, keeping only data relevant for analysis and evolution. This reduces storage costs and improves interface usability.

Strategic Summary

Managing models professionally is the foundation of maturity in Machine Learning projects. Without tracking, versioning, and execution control, models become opaque and unreliable artifacts, impossible to audit, maintain, or evolve with confidence. Using platforms like MLflow brings visibility, organization, and governance to this process—turning loose experimentation into dependable operation. Every logged experiment, versioned model, and documented artifact is a step toward building robust, secure, and scalable Machine Learning engineering. By mastering the fundamentals of model management, you establish the technical foundation that will support every future stage of your AI pipeline.

CHAPTER 3. MLFLOW ARCHITECTURE AND COMPONENTS

Building Machine Learning pipelines in professional environments requires a level of organization that goes beyond statistical modeling. It's necessary to orchestrate tools, data, code, artifacts, and metrics in a systematic, auditable, and extensible way. MLflow was designed to act as this central nervous system, coordinating different phases and functions across the model lifecycle. The key to its robustness lies in its modular architecture: each component solves a specific problem, but all work together with fluidity and coherence. Understanding this structure is essential for configuring and adapting MLflow to your team's real-world needs and operations.

MLflow's architecture is divided into four major components: Tracking, Projects, Models, and Model Registry. Together, they make up an ecosystem that covers everything from initial development to deployment and model governance in production. This separation of responsibilities enables modularity, scalability, and flexibility. Users can choose to use only one component or all, integrating them gradually into other enterprise systems. By understanding the function of each module, it becomes possible to design solutions that are simple enough for small teams and robust enough to meet corporate demands.

MLflow Tracking

MLflow Tracking is the core for experiment tracking. It allows the logging of runs, storing of parameters, saving of obtained metrics, storing of generated artifacts (such as models, validation files, graphs, logs), and even linking source code to the execution. This comprehensive logging turns each run into a structured, comparable, and auditable object.

By default, Tracking stores data locally in a .mlruns directory but can also be configured to use a remote server with a relational database and distributed file system. This flexibility allows you to start simple and scale without code changes.

Key elements:

- **Experiments** – Group multiple runs with a common goal.

- **Runs** – Each execution logged with parameters, metrics, and artifacts.

- **Tags** – Allow categorization of runs with useful metadata.

- **UI** – Interactive web interface for inspecting and comparing runs.

Integration with libraries like Scikit-learn, PyTorch, XGBoost, or LightGBM can be done manually (with mlflow.log_param(), mlflow.log_metric()) or automatically using wrappers like mlflow.sklearn.autolog().

MLflow Projects

The MLflow Projects module sets conventions for structuring Machine Learning projects in a reproducible way. It defines how to organize files, describe the required environment, and execute the main scripts, whether locally or remotely. This standardization solves the common issue of "it works on my machine, but not on yours."

MLflow identifies a project through a file named MLproject,

which acts as a manifest. This file declares:

- Project name

- Execution environment (Conda or Docker)

- Expected parameters

- Main execution command

With this setup, anyone with MLflow installed can clone the project repository and run it with a simple mlflow run command, without manually setting up libraries or dependencies.

Projects advantages:

- Reduced friction between science and engineering teams

- CI/CD automation facilitation

- Compatibility with distributed execution

Projects can also be integrated with version control tools like Git, enabling exact tracking of the code version used in each execution logged by Tracking.

MLflow Models

MLflow Models handles the standardization of saving and reusing trained models. When saving a model with mlflow.<flavor>.log_model(), it is automatically packaged into a format compatible with multiple deployment platforms. Each saved model contains:

- Code to load it

- Environment dependencies

- Prediction input/output definitions

- Supporting files (tokenizers, pipelines, etc.)

This packaged model can be loaded into any compatible environment, served as a REST API using mlflow models serve, or exported to platforms like Azure ML, SageMaker, Databricks, Kubernetes, and more.

Flavors are compatibility standards. A model can be saved with multiple flavors simultaneously—for example, a Scikit-learn model can be saved with both python_function and sklearn flavors, allowing it to be loaded by any tool compatible with MLflow's generic API or Scikit-learn's specific interface.

Useful features:

- Local deployment with mlflow models serve

- Docker container export

- Conversion to ONNX, PyFunc, Java, R

The goal is to make the trained model a portable, reusable asset independent of the environment in which it was created.

Model Registry

The Model Registry acts as a versioned model management system. It logs each saved model, stores its versions, enables technical comments, defines stages, and establishes a formal approval flow.

This repository centralizes control and offers visibility into what's in production, testing, or deprecated. Each registered version can have:

- Assigned stage (None, Staging, Production, Archived)

- Internal documentation and comments

- Transition history

- Links to the runs that originated the model

This granular control simplifies deployment and rollback, enables detailed auditing, and fosters collaboration across teams. With the Registry, MLOps teams can apply DevOps best practices like automated promotion, regression testing, and continuous validation.

CI/CD integration is direct: promoting a model to production can trigger a script that deploys the new version, updates the API, restarts services, and validates endpoint integrity.

Component Integration

Although each component works independently, MLflow's strength lies in their integrated use. The complete workflow connects as follows:

- A structured project with MLproject is run using mlflow run.

- During execution, parameters and metrics are logged via Tracking.

- At the end, the trained model is saved using mlflow.log_model().

- This model is automatically versioned in the Registry.

- If approved, it can be served with mlflow models serve or exported.

- The entire cycle is documented, auditable, and reproducible.

This integration creates a full trail from idea to production, enabling different teams to work at different stages of the process with complete visibility. A data scientist can train the model, an MLOps engineer can deploy it, a manager can monitor metrics, and the compliance team can audit every step.

Common Errors and Solutions

Error: "MLproject file not found"
Probable Cause: Executing a project without the manifest.
Recommended Solution: Create the MLproject file with keys name, conda_env, entry_points.

Error: "Flavor not recognized" when saving model
Probable Cause: Attempting to save with an unsupported flavor.
Recommended Solution: Check the library used and ensure compatibility with supported flavors (mlflow.sklearn, mlflow.pyfunc, etc.).

Error: "Cannot transition model to Production"
Probable Cause: Missing permissions in the Model Registry.
Recommended Solution: Grant user permissions or adjust the authentication configuration of the backend store.

Error: "Artifact storage permission denied"
Probable Cause: Path or bucket lacks write access.
Recommended Solution: Check --default-artifact-root configuration and storage access credentials.

Best Practices

- Use consistent naming for runs, models, and parameters—

avoid obscure or generic abbreviations.

- Version environments with Conda or Docker, always saving the specification alongside the project.

- Automate project execution with mlflow run from CI/CD pipelines to ensure reproducibility.

- Save models with multiple flavors when possible to maximize portability.

- Use the Model Registry as a single source of truth, avoiding multiple copies in different directories.

- Create formal stage transition policies with mandatory tests before promoting to Production.

- Integrate deployment with observability systems and alerts to monitor the active model continuously.

Strategic Summary

MLflow's modular architecture was designed to precisely and clearly cover every stage of the Machine Learning model lifecycle. Each component plays a specific and valuable role: Tracking organizes experiments, Projects ensures reproducibility, Models standardizes model packaging, and the Registry ensures version control and governance. When used together, these modules transform isolated experimentation into a continuous, auditable, and scalable operation.

CHAPTER 4. INSTALLATION AND ENVIRONMENT CONFIGURATION

Effective adoption of MLflow begins with a critical step: proper installation and environment configuration. This phase, often underestimated, has a direct impact on experiment fluency, result traceability, and integration with other systems in the data stack. A poorly configured environment can lead to hard-to-debug inconsistencies, log loss, authentication failures, and even the inability to reproduce models. Therefore, this stage must be treated with the same technical rigor applied to model development.

MLflow was designed for flexibility. It can be installed locally, used on remote servers, embedded in notebooks, or integrated into CI/CD pipelines. It can also be configured with different types of backends and artifact storage, allowing the tool to adapt to the constraints and objectives of each project. This versatility demands conscious decisions when setting up the environment, considering factors like scalability, persistence, security, and maintainability.

The basic installation of MLflow can be done with a single command:

bash

```
pip install mlflow
```

This installation enables the CLI (mlflow), the tracking and logging modules, model flavors, the local web server, and the ability to run projects. However, for professional use, it is necessary to complement this installation with the configuration of a backend store, artifact store, and appropriate environment variables.

Backend Store: Execution Control

The backend store is responsible for storing experiment metadata: parameters, metrics, tags, experiment names, and artifact references. By default, MLflow uses a local directory with .sqlite files, which is sufficient for testing and individual projects. For team usage or robust persistence, it is ideal to configure a relational database like PostgreSQL, MySQL, or a compatible managed service.

Model PostgreSQL connection string:

bash

```
export MLFLOW_TRACKING_URI=postgresql://
user:password@host:port/dbname
```

The database must be created in advance, and the user must have appropriate read and write permissions. The table structure is generated automatically on the first run.

Artifact Store: File Persistence

The artifact store keeps files associated with runs: trained models, images, log files, reports, and any other type of artifact. Locally, these files are saved in subfolders within the .mlruns directory. In corporate environments, it is recommended to use external systems like Amazon S3, Google Cloud Storage, or Azure Blob.

Configuration with S3:

bash

```
mlflow server \
```

```
--backend-store-uri postgresql://user:pass@host/db \
--default-artifact-root s3://my-bucket/mlflow \
--host 0.0.0.0 --port 5000
```

This separation between metadata and physical files increases robustness. It allows, for example, horizontal scaling of the backend and isolating the storage layer, optimizing costs and security.

Running the MLflow Tracking Server

The MLflow server can be started manually with the following command:

bash

```
mlflow server \
  --backend-store-uri <DATABASE_URI> \
  --default-artifact-root <STORAGE_URI> \
  --host 0.0.0.0 \
  --port 5000
```

This server provides a full REST interface and an interactive web interface accessible via browser. It can be secured with authentication via reverse proxy (like NGINX) or integrated with the company's authentication services.

Execution can be backgrounded using nohup, tmux, systemd, or any service orchestrator to ensure continuous availability.

Installation with Conda and virtualenv

It is highly recommended to install MLflow within isolated virtual environments. This avoids conflicts with system libraries and allows maintaining specific dependency versions.

Conda:

bash

```
conda create -n mlflow-env python=3.10
conda activate mlflow-env
pip install mlflow
```

Virtualenv:

bash

```
python -m venv mlflow-env
source mlflow-env/bin/activate
pip install mlflow
```

Virtual environments should be replicable. To ensure this, always export requirements with pip freeze > requirements.txt or conda env export > environment.yml, saving these files in the project repository.

Installing with Support for Specific Model Libraries

If the project uses specific libraries such as Scikit-learn, PyTorch, TensorFlow, or XGBoost, ensure the MLflow environment includes those libraries, since model saving and loading depends on the corresponding flavors.

For Scikit-learn:

bash

```
pip install scikit-learn
```

PyTorch:

bash

```
pip install torch
```

When saving a model using mlflow.sklearn.log_model() or mlflow.pytorch.log_model(), **MLflow** creates a standardized directory structure containing model serialization, dependencies, prediction code, and support files.

Remote Persistence: Advantages and Precautions

Working with remote backend and artifact stores requires attention to credentials, latency, and security policies. Never include usernames and passwords directly in the code. Use environment variables, .env files, or secret management systems like AWS Secrets Manager, Azure Key Vault, or HashiCorp Vault.

Also ensure that remote buckets or directories have version control enabled, encryption at rest, and minimally restrictive access policies. Experiment tracking is a strategic business asset and should be protected accordingly.

Integration with Notebooks

MLflow can be used directly within Jupyter or Google Colab notebooks. Just import the modules and log experiments with simple commands:

python

```
import mlflow


mlflow.set_tracking_uri("http://my-server:5000")

mlflow.set_experiment("classification_experiment")


with mlflow.start_run():
    mlflow.log_param("max_depth", 5)
```

```
mlflow.log_metric("accuracy", 0.92)
mlflow.sklearn.log_model(trained_model,
"classifier_model")
```

At the end of the execution, the experiment will be available in the server's web interface, with all data logged.

Common Errors and Solutions

Error: "Connection refused when setting tracking URI"
Probable Cause: MLflow server is inactive or blocked on the network.
Recommended Solution: Check if the service is running and if the host/port are accessible. Test with curl or telnet.

Error: "Permission denied writing to artifact location"
Probable Cause: Missing write permissions on the remote bucket or directory.
Recommended Solution: Check IAM policies, access keys, and folder permissions.

Error: mlflow.exceptions.RestException:
RESOURCE_ALREADY_EXISTS
Probable Cause: Attempt to create an experiment with an existing name.
Recommended   Solution: Use
mlflow.get_experiment_by_name() before creating a new experiment.

Error: "Cannot import mlflow" after activating the environment
Probable Cause: Virtual environment not activated correctly.
Recommended Solution: Reactivate the environment with conda activate or source, and reinstall the package.

Error: "No module named psycopg2" when using PostgreSQL
Probable Cause: Required driver dependency not installed.

Recommended Solution: Run pip install psycopg2-binary in the active environment.

Best Practices

- Create a separate repository for MLflow configuration, containing installation scripts, environment files, and usage documentation.

- Use .env or .bashrc to automatically load MLFLOW_TRACKING_URI and MLFLOW_ARTIFACT_ROOT variables.

- Protect MLflow server access with authentication and IP restriction, especially in cloud environments.

- Monitor remote storage usage and perform periodic cleanups of obsolete artifacts.

- Centralize logs using observability tools (like ELK, Grafana, Datadog) to track failures and performance.

- Clearly document the installation and environment replication process, including step-by-step instructions for new team members.

Strategic Summary

Proper configuration of the MLflow environment is not a secondary step—it is the foundation upon which all experiment engineering will be built. A solid environment ensures traceability, secure collaboration, scalable operations, and reduced operational errors. Knowing how to install, isolate, secure, and connect MLflow components defines the difference between a functional tool and a professional engineering platform. With a well-configured foundation, each future experiment will be more reliable, each model more accessible, and each decision backed by verifiable technical groundwork. This is the basis of modern Machine Learning engineering, and where true mastery begins.

CHAPTER 5. EXPERIMENT TRACKING

Tracking Machine Learning experiments is not an accessory activity — it is the core of operational maturity in data science projects. When teams fail to systematically document parameters, metrics, and artifacts, the consequences are immediate: models become irreproducible, improvements are made blindly, and superior results are forgotten or lost. Experiment tracking is the mechanism that organizes, standardizes, and historicizes the entire machine learning process. With MLflow, this traceability is elevated to a professional level, offering accessible interfaces, complete logging, and seamless integration into development workflows.

Tracking allows each pipeline execution to be recorded as a complete information block: which parameters were used, which metrics were obtained, what model was saved, which files were generated, and what code was associated. This structure creates an auditable and comparable trail. Without tracking, there is no control over technical evolution and no objective basis for deciding which model to deploy or why one version outperformed another.

The MLflow Tracking module consists of three main blocks: experiments, runs, and artifacts. Each experiment groups runs related to a common goal. Each run represents a training attempt with specific parameters. Artifacts are the objects associated with the process — log files, charts, sampled datasets, saved models, and everything else relevant for understanding or reusing that run.

Setting up tracking is simple. Just point to the MLflow server URI (local or remote) and start an experiment. From there, each run can be explicitly started, logged, and ended. The web interface displays results in a comparative way, enabling visual analysis, parameter-based filtering, and even data export.

python

```python
import mlflow

mlflow.set_tracking_uri("http://my-server:5000")
mlflow.set_experiment("credit_classification")

with mlflow.start_run():
    mlflow.log_param("max_depth", 4)
    mlflow.log_param("learning_rate", 0.1)
    mlflow.log_metric("accuracy", 0.85)
    mlflow.sklearn.log_model(model, "credit_model")
```

This code block logs all data related to the run: parameters like max_depth, the accuracy metric, and the trained model. All of this becomes available in the graphical interface for comparison.

The separation between parameters and metrics is fundamental. Parameters are controlled inputs — hyperparameter values, algorithm choices, batch sizes, imputation methods. Metrics are measured results — accuracy, F1-score, training time, AUC, etc. This distinction helps organize experimental reasoning by separating input decisions from observed outputs.

MLflow also supports the use of tags, which act as additional metadata. They are useful for classifying runs by author, reference date, code branch, or any other relevant criterion for the team.

Tracking can be manual (with explicit log function calls) or automatic using mlflow.autolog(). This function detects the framework in use (such as Scikit-learn, TensorFlow, or XGBoost) and automatically logs parameters, metrics, and models based on pipeline objects.

python

```
import mlflow.sklearn
mlflow.sklearn.autolog()
```

With autologging, there's no need to write log commands line by line. Execution is tracked in the background, and the data is organized in a standardized way.

In addition to parameters and metrics, you can log artifacts — physical files. This includes validation charts, CSV files with predictions, input data samples, or any other relevant output. These are saved using mlflow.log_artifact().

python

```
mlflow.log_artifact("distribution_chart.png")
```

These files become associated with the run and can be downloaded through the web interface, inspected by other team members, or used in later analysis. The ability to store artifacts makes MLflow a dynamic technical repository.

Another important function is mlflow.log_dict(), which allows saving Python objects as JSON dictionaries. It's useful for logging complex configurations, class mappings, reports, or structured results.

python

```
advanced_metrics = {"precision": 0.88, "recall": 0.81, "f1": 0.845}
mlflow.log_dict(advanced_metrics, "metrics_report.json")
```

Experiments can be visualized through the web interface by accessing the MLflow server address. Each experiment appears as a group of runs, which can be filtered by parameters, sorted by metrics, or inspected individually. The interface displays interactive comparison charts, making it easier to choose the best model based on multiple criteria.

Beyond the web interface, tracking can be accessed programmatically via REST API or the mlflow.tracking library. This allows for custom dashboards, automatic reporting, or internal systems to be fed with experiment data.

python

```
from mlflow.tracking import MlflowClient

client = MlflowClient()
runs = client.search_runs(experiment_ids=["1"],
order_by=["metrics.f1 DESC"])
```

This command retrieves the runs from experiment ID 1, ordered by F1 score. This feature is powerful in automated pipelines, where the best model can be programmatically selected and deployed based on updated metrics.

Common Errors and Solutions

Error: "Active run already exists"
Probable Cause: Attempt to start a run within another without proper closure.

Recommended Solution: Ensure mlflow.end_run() is called after each start_run(), especially in loops or nested functions.

Error: "Failed to log param: duplicate key"
Probable Cause: Attempting to log a parameter with the same name twice.
Recommended Solution: Check the code and standardize parameter names to avoid duplication.

Error: "Logging artifact failed: file not found"
Probable Cause: Incorrect file path or file not generated before logging.
Recommended Solution: Validate that the file exists on the local system before logging it as an artifact.

Error: "Experiment with name already exists"
Probable Cause: Repeated creation of an experiment with the same name.
Recommended Solution: Use mlflow.set_experiment() instead of create_experiment() to avoid conflicts.

Error: "Tracking URI not set"
Probable Cause: MLflow doesn't know where to send the data.
Recommended Solution: Set MLFLOW_TRACKING_URI as an environment variable or use mlflow.set_tracking_uri() in code.

Best Practices

- Always start each run with start_run() and end with end_run(), even in notebooks or automated pipelines.

- Use descriptive and standardized parameter names to facilitate comparison between runs.

- Log all relevant metrics, not just the main one. This allows for more comprehensive analysis and tracking of side effects from changes.

- Save models, reports, and charts as artifacts. This turns each run into a complete and self-explanatory object.

- Avoid using dynamic or random values in run names. Prefer tags and metadata to differentiate runs more reliably.

- Use autolog() when possible, but complement it manually with additional logs that autolog doesn't capture (like custom artifacts).

- Maintain a naming convention for experiments, indicating project, task, and scope (e.g., fraud_xgboost_tuning).

- Store experiments in a remote backend with file versioning enabled to ensure reproducibility and security.

- Automate the cleanup of old or obsolete runs, but only after backup and relevance analysis.

Strategic Summary

Experiment tracking is the technical foundation that transforms data science into applied engineering. With it, every attempt is documented, every parameter is comparable, and every model is justifiable. MLflow Tracking offers a simple and powerful structure to ensure this control, with flexibility for individual or team use, local or cloud-based, manual or automated. Mastering tracking is the first step to creating auditable, scalable, and collaborative pipelines, where decisions are based on concrete technical evidence — not vague guesswork. This is where reliable Machine Learning engineering begins: by logging, analyzing, and learning from every experiment.

CHAPTER 6. ARTIFACT AND RESOURCE HANDLING

Every Machine Learning run generates a set of technical evidence that must be stored, organized, and retrieved precisely. Trained models, metric reports, charts, data samples, log files, and intermediate scripts are fundamental pieces to ensure reproducibility and technical evolution of a project. These objects are called *artifacts*. Proper artifact management enables teams to audit, version, share, and reuse results with confidence and speed. MLflow treats artifact handling as a native function integrated into its tracking ecosystem, logging everything a run produces in an accessible and structured way.

Artifacts may take different formats and serve multiple purposes. Some are automatically generated by the pipeline —such as saved models, validation files, checkpoints—while others are created as part of complementary analyses or experiment documentation. Regardless of origin, every artifact should be logged and associated with the corresponding run, creating a complete trail of the logic that led to the final result.

MLflow provides multiple functions for logging, accessing, and retrieving artifacts. The most direct is mlflow.log_artifact(), which saves any file in the context of the active run. It can be used for individual files or entire directories.

python

```
import mlflow

mlflow.log_artifact("evaluation_report.pdf")
```

When run within an execution block, the file evaluation_report.pdf is saved in the artifact repository associated with the current run. It can be downloaded, viewed, and reused at any time.

You can also save entire directories using the log_artifacts() function:

python

```
mlflow.log_artifacts("outputs/")
```

This allows you to store complete sets of related files, such as training-generated charts, CSV files with prediction samples, or transformation scripts applied to the data.

In addition to physical files, MLflow also supports logging structured objects like dictionaries, lists, and JSON objects. The mlflow.log_dict() function automatically converts the structure into a .json file and stores it as an artifact.

python

```
results = {
    "precision": 0.84,
    "recall": 0.79,
    "f1": 0.81
}
mlflow.log_dict(results, "advanced_metrics.json")
```

This type of logging is extremely useful for capturing composite results, run configurations, class mappings, feature weights, or any other hierarchically structured data.

Another available resource is mlflow.log_text(), ideal for saving strings such as custom logs, experiment notes, alerts, or technical validation messages.

python

```
mlflow.log_text("Model trained with balanced dataset", "notes.txt")
```

All these artifacts are stored in the directory defined by --default-artifact-root, which can be local or remote. In professional environments, it's recommended to configure buckets in services like Amazon S3, Azure Blob, or GCS to ensure redundancy, access control, and scalability.

Artifacts can later be accessed via MLflow's graphical interface, direct URLs, manual download, or programmatically using the MLflow Client API:

python

```
from mlflow.tracking import MlflowClient

client = MlflowClient()

run_id = "b349fa98d56c4760b716932157"

client.download_artifacts(run_id, "evaluation_report.pdf", dst_path="./")
```

This integration allows automation of artifact retrieval in validation scripts, final reports, audit notebooks, or internal monitoring systems. It's also possible to use artifact paths for integration with external tools such as dashboards, evidence repositories, version control, or backups.

In addition to explicit artifacts, MLflow also logs implicit artifacts when saving models with mlflow.log_model(). Each saved model generates a directory containing:

- Serialization file (pickle, h5, etc.)

- MLmodel file with model metadata

- conda.yaml file with environment dependencies

- Prediction code (in PyFunc format or specific flavor)

- Any sub-artifact used in model construction

This complete package ensures that the model can be re-imported, re-executed, and reused identically to the original context. It also enables export to REST APIs, containers, external systems, or automated production pipelines.

To save multiple models in a single run, simply name each one distinctly:

python

mlflow.sklearn.log_model(model1, "logistic_model")

mlflow.sklearn.log_model(model2, "random_forest_model")

Each model directory will be versioned and referenced separately, making later comparison and A/B testing easier.

Common Errors and Solutions

Error: "FileNotFoundError: file does not exist"
Probable Cause: Attempting to log a file that hasn't been created or is saved in the wrong directory.
Recommended Solution: Ensure the file exists before calling log_artifact() by using os.path.exists() as a pre-check.

Error: "Permission denied writing to artifact store"
Probable Cause: Restricted access to remote bucket or invalid path.
Recommended Solution: Check S3/Blob permissions and validate authentication variables or IAM policies.

Error: "Artifact path too long"
Probable Cause: File or subdirectory names are too long.
Recommended Solution: Use short, standardized names and avoid excessive folder nesting.

Error: "Invalid artifact type"
Probable Cause: Attempting to log unsupported objects directly (e.g., raw pandas objects).
Recommended Solution: Convert to an appropriate format like CSV, JSON, or Pickle before saving.

Error: "Overwriting existing artifact"
Probable Cause: Repeated logging with the same file name and path.
Recommended Solution: Include a timestamp or UUID in file names to ensure uniqueness.

Best Practices

- Save all relevant files produced during a run, even if they are not used directly in the final model.

- Organize artifacts into directories by category (charts, logs, results, models) for easier future navigation.

- Include unique identifiers in artifact names to prevent collisions and support cross-referencing.

- Automate the generation of files like reports, tables, images, and log all of them as artifacts at the end of execution.

- Validate logging success and capture exceptions to avoid data loss in automated pipelines.

- Document in each artifact the context of its creation — code version, branch, author, date, and experimental config.

- Use compression (.zip, .tar.gz) for large file sets or many small files sharing context.

- Integrate artifact retrieval with continuous evaluation scripts, dashboards, and quality systems.

Strategic Summary

Mastering artifact handling transforms MLflow into much more than a metric tracker — it becomes a technical intelligence repository, a vault of evidence documenting every step of Machine Learning engineering. Artifacts are the bridge between execution and a project's technical memory — they enable reuse, ensure auditability, accelerate onboarding of new members, and shield the team from knowledge loss. Learning to efficiently log, organize, and retrieve artifacts is a strategic skill. This is what turns a simple run into a reliable, verifiable asset ready to scale.

CHAPTER 7. INTRODUCTION TO MLPROJECTS

As Machine Learning projects evolve, they become more complex and begin to rely on multiple libraries, specific execution environments, variable parameters, and data structures that must be handled with precision. Reproducing the same experiment on different machines with distinct configurations often leads to hard-to-diagnose errors. It's common for code to work perfectly on the author's machine but fail in production servers, collaborative environments, or automated pipelines. The MLflow Projects module was created to solve exactly this problem: standardizing how Machine Learning projects are packaged, executed, and reproduced, regardless of the environment.

MLflow Projects defines a simple yet powerful convention. It specifies how a project should be structured, what environment it requires, which parameters are available, and what main command should be executed. This allows anyone with MLflow installed to run a project with a single command—even if they've never seen the code before.

The basic structure of an MLflow project is composed of two main elements:

- A directory with the project files

- A file called MLproject that acts as the project manifest

This manifest is written in YAML and contains essential

metadata. Its main function is to ensure reproducibility by explicitly declaring everything the project needs to run correctly.

A typical MLproject file follows this structure:

yaml

```
name: credit_classification


conda_env: conda.yaml


entry_points:
  main:
    parameters:
      learning_rate: {type: float, default: 0.01}
      max_depth: {type: int, default: 5}
    command: >
      python train.py --learning_rate {learning_rate} --max_depth {max_depth}
```

- name defines the project name

- conda_env specifies the Conda environment to use

- entry_points defines executable entry points with parameters

With this structure, running the project on any machine is as simple as:

bash

```
mlflow run https://github.com/user/mlflow-project -P
learning_rate=0.1 -P max_depth=7
```

MLflow will:

- Clone the repository

- Create (or activate) the Conda environment defined in conda.yaml

- Substitute the parameters into the command

- Execute the main script with the given settings

This standardization drastically reduces errors caused by missing dependencies, version conflicts, or improperly passed parameters. It also facilitates integration with automation pipelines, CI/CD systems, continuous validation, and orchestration tools like Airflow or Kubeflow.

Environment definition is another key pillar. MLflow Projects supports two main ways to define environments:

- conda_env – for Python-based projects using Conda

- docker_env – for projects running in Docker containers

When using conda_env, a conda.yaml file must be provided, listing all libraries required by the project:

yaml

name: credit_classification_env

channels:

  - defaults

```
dependencies:
  - python=3.10
  - scikit-learn
  - pandas
  - matplotlib
  - pip:
      - mlflow
```

MLflow will create the environment based on this file before execution. This ensures that all experiments run with the same libraries, preventing inconsistent results caused by version mismatches or undocumented packages.

When using docker_env, the manifest includes the definition of the Docker image to be used:

yaml

```
docker_env:
  image: user/mlflow-base:latest
```

This format is useful in production environments or clusters, where containers guarantee full isolation and execution consistency.

The entry_points defined in MLproject can contain multiple commands, allowing a single project to support different routines such as training, validation, exploratory analysis, deployment, and more. Each can be run separately:

bash

```
mlflow run . -e exploratory_analysis
```

Additionally, MLflow Projects supports remote execution. Projects can be run locally, on a remote machine via SSH, or even in a cluster. You just need to configure the appropriate executor and pass the required arguments. This enables task distribution, parallel execution, and complex workflow orchestration with ease.

Another important point is that parameters passed via command line or script are automatically logged in tracking, reinforcing experiment traceability. Each run will be documented with the exact parameters used, linked to the code and environment.

Common Errors and Solutions

Error: "MLproject file not found"
Probable Cause: Project directory does not contain the required manifest.
Recommended Solution: Create an MLproject file at the project root, following correct YAML syntax.

Error: "Unknown parameter" when running the project
Probable Cause: Parameter passed with -P is not defined in the corresponding entry_point.
Recommended Solution: Check the parameters section in the MLproject file and ensure all names are aligned.

Error: "Conda environment build failed"
Probable Cause: conda.yaml file has syntax errors or incompatible dependencies.
Recommended Solution: Validate the file manually by running conda env create -f conda.yaml before running with MLflow.

Error: "Entry point not found"
Probable Cause: Attempt to run an entry point with an incorrect name.

Recommended Solution: Check the names defined in the entry_points section and use exactly as declared.

Error: "Permission denied when executing script"
Probable Cause: Script file lacks execution permission.
Recommended Solution: Use chmod +x on the main script or ensure the interpreter (python) is correctly specified in the command.

Best Practices

- Always use MLproject files, even for small projects. It disciplines the team and prepares code for scaling or integrating with more complex pipelines.

- Name entry points clearly, representing actual project tasks (e.g., train, evaluate, serve).

- Document parameters in the manifest with types and default values to simplify execution and reduce errors.

- Include validations in the main script to ensure parameters fall within expected ranges.

- Use frozen Conda environments with specific versions of each library to prevent compatibility issues.

- Validate both conda.yaml and MLproject files before pushing to the repository to ensure the project can run without intervention.

- Keep the main code modular, with reusable functions and a clear separation between training, evaluation, and logging logic.

- Integrate MLflow Projects with Git version control to trace each run to its corresponding commit.

- Automate executions using mlflow run inside CI/CD scripts like GitHub Actions, GitLab CI, Jenkins, or similar.

- Use Docker images only when necessary—Conda environments are faster to set up and easier to debug.

Strategic Summary

The introduction to MLflow Projects marks a turning point in how Machine Learning projects are structured and executed. With a simple YAML-based convention, it transforms isolated experiments into reproducible, auditable, and scalable workflows. The MLproject manifest acts as a technical contract that standardizes environments, defines parameters, and organizes executions. It reduces dependency on manual instructions, eliminates ambiguity between team members, and allows projects to evolve securely and traceably.

CHAPTER 8. MLFLOW MODELS

Machine Learning models are not merely end-products of a series of experiments—they are assets that must be versioned, reused, deployed, and audited over time. The way these models are saved, loaded, and transferred across environments directly impacts the reliability of a solution's lifecycle. The MLflow Models module was created to standardize this handling, allowing trained models to be consistently packaged with all necessary information for future reuse, production deployment, or integration with external systems.

The concept of a model in MLflow goes beyond the serialized object. Each registered model includes metadata, prediction code, execution environment, and support for multiple formats. This modular structure makes models portable across languages, tools, and infrastructures—without the need for manual adjustments or rework.

The technical foundation of this approach is the **model directory** generated with each log_model() call. When a model is saved with MLflow, a new directory is created with the following structure:

- Root directory with the model name

- MLmodel file specifying the flavor and entry commands

- conda.yaml file listing environment dependencies

- Serialization file (e.g., model.pkl, model.h5, etc.)

- Additional subdirectories depending on the model type or included artifacts

The MLmodel file is the central component of this structure. It describes the model's flavor(s), i.e., the frameworks it is compatible with, and also points to the file path and prediction method.

yaml

```yaml
flavors:
  python_function:
    loader_module: mlflow.sklearn
    data: model.pkl
    env: conda.yaml
  sklearn:
    pickled_model: model.pkl
    sklearn_version: 1.1.3
```

The presence of multiple **flavors** allows the same model to be used by different systems. The python_function flavor is a generic interface compatible with MLflow's REST API, while flavors like sklearn, pytorch, xgboost, or keras indicate native compatibility with those specific frameworks.

Saving a model with MLflow is straightforward. For a model trained with Scikit-learn, the process follows this pattern:

python

```python
import mlflow.sklearn


mlflow.sklearn.log_model(model, "credit_model")
```

This command logs the current model, saving the complete structure including the .pkl file, environment definition, and metadata. The directory credit_model is created in the artifact store linked to the current run.

To load the model later—whether in another script, pipeline, or production system—the process is equally simple:

python

```
loaded_model = mlflow.sklearn.load_model("runs:/<run_id>/
credit_model")
```

This command retrieves the model logged in a previous run and loads the corresponding Python object, ready for use with new data.

When using the python_function flavor, the model can be loaded in a framework-agnostic way:

python

```
from mlflow.pyfunc import load_model


generic_model = load_model("runs:/<run_id>/credit_model")
predictions = generic_model.predict(new_data)
```

This is useful for encapsulating prediction logic without exposing the underlying framework. It is also the required format for serving the model as a REST API using:

bash

```
mlflow models serve -m runs:/<run_id>/credit_model -p 1234
```

This command starts a local server that exposes an HTTP endpoint for making predictions. Just send a JSON payload to get a direct response.

Beyond saving and loading models locally, MLflow allows registering models in a central repository using the

Model Registry. To do so, use mlflow.register_model():

python

```
from mlflow.register_model import register_model


register_model("runs:/<run_id>/credit_model",
"CreditClassifier")
```

This command adds the model to the registry, initiating version control and enabling transitions between stages like *Staging*, *Production*, and *Archived*. This structure simplifies version management, approvals, and rollbacks.

Registered models can be referenced using URIs such as models:/CreditClassifier/Production, which simplifies production scripts needing the latest approved version.

MLflow Models also supports exporting to formats like **ONNX, SparkML**, and **TensorFlow SavedModel**. This expands deployment and integration possibilities, especially for industrial pipelines, embedded applications, or GPU-based services.

Each flavor has specific methods to log and load the model, always adhering to the metadata structure defined by MLflow. Examples include:

python

mlflow.xgboost.log_model()

mlflow.pytorch.log_model()

mlflow.keras.log_model()

mlflow.sklearn.log_model()

This variety enables MLflow to act as a **unifying layer** across multiple frameworks, simplifying model control even in teams that use different approaches.

Common Errors and Solutions

Error: "ModuleNotFoundError when loading model"
Probable Cause: Execution environment lacks required model dependencies.
Recommended Solution: Load the model in an environment using the same conda.yaml generated during log_model(), or recreate it with mlflow models prepare-env.

Error: "Model flavor not found"
Probable Cause: Model saved with a specific flavor and loaded using a generic function.
Recommended Solution: Use the load_model function corresponding to the flavor used during logging.

Error: "ValueError: Model URI is not valid"
Probable Cause: Malformed or incorrect model URI.
Recommended Solution: Use runs:/<run_id>/<path> for unregistered models or models:/<name>/<stage> for models in the registry.

Error: "Incompatible model version" during deployment
Probable Cause: Version mismatch between MLflow used for logging and for loading.
Recommended Solution: Update the MLflow installation to ensure compatibility.

Error: "Permission denied when saving model"
Probable Cause: Lack of write permissions in the artifact store.
Recommended Solution: Check authentication variables, IAM policies, or local directory permissions.

Best Practices

- Save all models with consistent and descriptive names to avoid name duplication and ease registry searches.

- Use multiple flavors whenever possible to ensure models are reusable in various contexts.

- Register relevant models in the Model Registry and apply formal versioning with defined stages.

- Document model purpose, dataset used, and primary metric within metadata and as an additional artifact.

- Create dedicated environments to load models using the conda.yaml file generated automatically.

- Use local deployment with mlflow models serve for testing and validation only—prefer production-grade orchestration tools for real deployments.

- Automate model logging, registration, and deployment as part of the CI/CD pipeline.

- Validate the integrity of loaded models before serving predictions in production, including input shape, data type, and expected structure.

- Include scripts for format conversion (e.g., ONNX) when interoperability with embedded systems or specialized

APIs is needed.

- Periodically audit registered models, archive outdated versions, and keep technical descriptions and use contexts updated.

Strategic Summary

The MLflow Models module redefines how Machine Learning models are managed throughout a project's lifecycle. By standardizing model saving, packaging, and recovery, it transforms a technical artifact into an operational product —ready to be reused, validated, and safely deployed. The combination of flavors, versioning, centralized registration, and multi-format compatibility provides engineering teams with a solid foundation for operating at scale, with governance and flexibility.

CHAPTER 9. MODEL REGISTRY

Deploying Machine Learning models in real-world environments requires much more than strong statistical performance. Clear processes for versioning, tracking, and governance are essential to ensure reliability, security, and auditability. Without these mechanisms, the risk of version inconsistencies, silent performance regressions, and operational failures increases significantly. MLflow's Model Registry was developed to address these challenges, providing a centralized model management structure with support for multiple versions, formal stages, and technical approval workflows.

The Model Registry acts as a control and organization layer over models saved using log_model(). Instead of dealing directly with scattered artifact directories, the Registry allows models to be registered in a central repository with a unique name, incremental versioning, and contextual information. This transforms a model from a simple serialized file into a technical object with identity, history, and deployment state.

Each model registered in the MLflow Registry receives a unique name and can contain multiple numbered versions. Each version can be assigned to one of the following stages:

- **None** – newly registered model, not yet formally reviewed

- **Staging** – version in validation, used in test or pre-production environments

- **Production** – active version, currently deployed in

production

- **Archived** – older or deprecated versions kept for historical or audit purposes

These stages serve as functional labels and allow process automation, such as automatic deployments, regression testing, rollback, and model approvals via technical review.

Registering a model in the Registry is simple. After logging the model with log_model(), use mlflow.register_model() to link it to the central repository:

python

```
from mlflow.register_model import register_model


model_uri = "runs:/<run_id>/credit_model"
registro = register_model(model_uri, "CreditClassifier")
```

This command creates a new model named CreditClassifier and registers the current version as number 1. Each new registration under the same name automatically increments the version.

Model versions can be viewed and managed via MLflow's web interface, REST API, or the MlflowClient library. Each registered version contains metadata such as:

- Run ID that originated the model

- User who registered it

- Registration timestamp

- Current stage

- Technical comments

- Associated tags

- Direct links to artifacts

This structure simplifies auditing and tracking the origin of each model, ensuring that any algorithmic decision can be technically investigated in depth.

Version promotion between stages can be done via the interface or through code:

python

```python
from mlflow.tracking import MlflowClient


client = MlflowClient()
client.transition_model_version_stage(
    name="CreditClassifier",
    version=3,
    stage="Production",
    archive_existing_versions=True
)
```

This command promotes version 3 to *Production*, optionally archiving all previous versions. This ensures that only one version is active at a time, reducing the risk of concurrent deployments or operational inconsistencies.

Technical comments can also be added to each version:

python

```
client.update_model_version(
    name="CreditClassifier",
    version=3,
    description="Model validated with updated March dataset"
)
```

These comments are visible in the web interface and can serve as living documentation, indicating promotion criteria, datasets used, validated metrics, or specific dependencies.

Another important feature is listing and searching registered models. This allows external systems or automated pipelines to query the Registry for the most up-to-date or suitable model for a specific task.

python

```
versions =
client.search_model_versions("name='CreditClassifier'")
for v in versions:
    print(v.version, v.current_stage, v.run_id)
```

This query returns all registered versions of a given model, their current stages, and associated run IDs. This enables automated decisions such as "fetch the latest version in Staging," "compare metrics across versions," or "rollback to the last valid version."

The Registry also supports deletion and archiving. A model can be retained for history even after being removed from production, ensuring that past decisions can be reconstructed if needed. In compliance-sensitive projects, this is a major strategic advantage.

The use of the Registry is particularly helpful in collaborative environments, where data scientists train models and MLOps engineers handle deployments. It acts as a formal transition point between development and production, offering technical control, auditable versioning, and operational traceability.

In addition to technical governance, the Registry enables standardized model consumption. Once registered, a model can be loaded anywhere using a standard URI:

python

```
production_model = mlflow.pyfunc.load_model("models:/
CreditClassifier/Production")
```

This URI retrieves the currently active version in the *Production* stage. It simplifies the construction of inference pipelines, APIs, services, and dashboards that always use the latest approved version—without manually updating the URI with every release.

This standardization also supports continuous validation systems, where a new model is automatically promoted to *Staging*, validated through automated tests, and promoted to *Production* only if it meets approval criteria. This flow integrates seamlessly into modern CI/CD systems and delivery pipelines.

Common Errors and Solutions

Error: "Model name already exists"
Probable Cause: Attempt to register a model with a name already in use.
Recommended Solution: Use unique names per model or reuse the existing name to create a new version.

Error: "Invalid stage transition"
Probable Cause: Attempt to move a model directly from None to *Production*.

Recommended Solution: Promote the model to Staging first, validate it, then transition to *Production*.

Error: "Run not found for model version"
Probable Cause: The associated run was deleted or is no longer accessible.
Recommended Solution: Keep associated runs as long as active versions exist in the Registry, and ensure proper backups.

Error: "Permission denied to transition stage"
Probable Cause: The current user lacks necessary permissions.
Recommended Solution: Adjust permissions in the backend or run with appropriate credentials.

Error: "Stage conflict: multiple versions in Production"
Probable Cause: Manual promotion without automatic archiving of previous versions.
Recommended Solution: Enable the parameter archive_existing_versions=True when promoting a new version.

Best Practices

- Use consistent and descriptive names for registered models, reflecting their function and technical scope.

- Document each version with clear comments, validated metrics, datasets used, and relevant annotations.

- Create formal promotion policies (e.g., require Staging validation via script or manual approval before Production).

- Automate model registration and stage transition as part of a complete CI/CD pipeline.

- Maintain only one active version at a time in Production to ensure delivery predictability.

- Archive older versions only after confirming they are no longer needed for rollback or comparison.

- Periodically audit registered models to ensure all have clear descriptions, origins, and usage definitions.

- Implement alerts and logs for all stage transitions to facilitate action tracking and accountability.

- Create dashboards to monitor model status, versions, and key metrics per stage.

- Integrate the Registry with deployment and orchestration tools to make promotion a functional step in the delivery process.

Strategic Summary

MLflow's Model Registry is the key to transforming trained models into reliable, governable, and traceable products. It provides the structure teams need to control the model lifecycle with the same discipline applied to software systems. By enabling versioning, stage promotion, technical documentation, and pipeline integration, the Registry creates a strong bridge between experimentation and production. It enables consistent deliveries, simplifies rollback in case of failure, ensures auditability, and organizes the model portfolio in a clear and sustainable way. Mastering its use means taking full technical control of model operations at scale.

CHAPTER 10. INTEGRATION WITH CI/CD PIPELINES

Machine Learning in production can no longer rely on manual runs, subjective decisions, or disconnected processes between experimentation and delivery. Models must be trained, validated, approved, and deployed with the same precision and automation applied to software development. Integration with CI/CD pipelines (Continuous Integration and Continuous Delivery) is the mechanism that transforms trained models into replicable, versionable, and reliable assets—with full traceability and automated deployment. MLflow provides all the building blocks needed to orchestrate this lifecycle, from tracking to controlled deployment, enabling teams to move fast without sacrificing governance.

The traditional CI/CD logic is based on three principles: automate, validate, and deliver. In software projects, this means running tests at every commit, building packages, checking for regressions, and deploying without manual intervention. In Machine Learning, the same logic applies to the model lifecycle. Every change in code, data, or hyperparameters should trigger a chain of events: train the model, evaluate performance, compare it to the current version, and decide whether to promote it to production.

MLflow fits naturally into this flow. Its components — **Tracking**, **Projects**, **Models**, and **Registry** — are designed to log executions, standardize environments, save versioned models, and control stage transitions. To integrate MLflow with CI/CD pipelines, these components must be connected to tools like

GitHub Actions, GitLab CI, Jenkins, Azure DevOps, or any other workflow automation system.

A CI/CD pipeline structure with MLflow typically follows this flow:

- Detect changes in the code or data repository

- Create or activate an isolated environment (Conda, Docker)

- Execute the project using mlflow run

- Log parameters, metrics, and artifacts via MLflow Tracking

- Compare results to previous versions

- Save and register the model with log_model() and register_model()

- Run automated validation tests

- Promote the model in the Registry to *Staging* or *Production*

- Deploy the model to a REST endpoint, microservice, or external system

This flow can be implemented modularly with separate scripts or monolithic pipelines, as long as it follows the principle of complete automation.

Using mlflow run, project execution becomes standardized. The repository must contain an MLproject file with defined parameters and environment. The CI/CD pipeline will clone the repository, read the manifest, and execute the task with parameters defined in the pipeline.

bash

```
mlflow run . -P learning_rate=0.01 -P n_estimators=100
```

Upon completion, results will be logged automatically—parameters, metrics, and artifacts stored in the configured backend. Each pipeline execution thus generates an auditable run with full traceability.

The generated model can be saved using `mlflow.sklearn.log_model()` or the corresponding flavor. After saving, the pipeline should include a technical validation step. This can be done through custom tests, expected metric thresholds, or regression validation scripts.

If the model passes the defined criteria, it can be registered and promoted in the Registry:

python

```
from mlflow.register_model import register_model

from mlflow.tracking import MlflowClient


registro = register_model("runs:/<run_id>/credit_model", "CreditClassifier")

client = MlflowClient()

client.transition_model_version_stage("CreditClassifier", version=registro.version, stage="Staging")
```

Automating this process ensures promotion is based on objective, logged criteria—eliminating subjectivity and increasing operational reliability.

Another critical point in CI/CD integration is automatic comparison with previous models. You can retrieve the last

Production version, load its metrics, and compare it with the current results. If the new model outperforms the previous one, it can be automatically promoted.

python

```
prod_model = client.get_latest_versions("CreditClassifier",
stages=["Production"])[0]

if new_accuracy > prod_model.accuracy:

    client.transition_model_version_stage("CreditClassifier",
version=registro.version, stage="Production",
archive_existing_versions=True)
```

This logic enables autonomous pipelines that not only train models but also make technical decisions based on measurable performance—turning model delivery into a closed, reliable cycle.

For deployment integration, MLflow natively supports REST endpoints via mlflow models serve. The pipeline can be configured so that, after model promotion, the service is restarted with the new version:

bash

```
mlflow models serve -m models:/CreditClassifier/Production -p
5000 --no-conda
```

This command starts an HTTP server with the active model. It can be coupled with a Docker service, Kubernetes, or any orchestration solution. The pipeline may include health checks, response validation, and autoscaling scripts.

Another deployment model is via Docker containers. MLflow allows exporting the model with an embedded server:

bash

```
mlflow models build-docker -m models:/CreditClassifier/
Production -n mlflow-classifier:latest
```

The pipeline can package the model, build the Docker image, and push it to a repository like Docker Hub, ECR, or GCR—ready to be deployed in production using tools like ArgoCD, Helm, or Terraform.

When building CI/CD integration, it's critical to ensure that all sensitive variables—like tracking URIs, storage credentials, or Registry access tokens—are protected. They should be stored as secure secrets in the CI/CD platform and loaded as environment variables during execution.

Common Errors and Solutions

Error: mlflow.exceptions.RestException: INVALID_PARAMETER_VALUE
Probable Cause: Pipeline attempts to register or promote model with incorrect parameters.
Recommended Solution: Validate parameter types and names according to Registry documentation before the call.

Error: "Docker image build failed"
Probable Cause: Lack of daemon permissions or model dependency incompatibility with the base image.
Recommended Solution: Ensure root permissions, active Docker daemon, and compatible base image for the model flavors used.

Error: "Model not found at specified URI"
Probable Cause: The model's associated run was not properly logged, or the ID is incorrect.
Recommended Solution: Wait for the run to finish before registering the model and verify the path is accessible in the configured backend.

Error: "Permission denied when transitioning model version stage"
Probable Cause: Unauthorized user attempting to manipulate Registry stages.
Recommended Solution: Check the authentication token's permissions or configure access rules in the MLflow backend.

Error: "Health check failed after deploy"
Probable Cause: The promoted model was deployed with input incompatibility.
Recommended Solution: Include a functional validation step in the pipeline using simulated data and response comparison before promoting the model.

Best Practices

- Structure the CI/CD pipeline into independent, named stages like *train, validate, register, promote, deploy*

- Automate unit and regression tests every time a new model is trained

- Store experiments in a remote, versioned backend, with separate storage for artifacts

- Maintain detailed log records for each pipeline stage to facilitate debugging and auditing

- Use consistent names and timestamps for saved models to enable cross-referencing between tracking, registry, and external systems

- Integrate MLflow with observability tools like Prometheus, Grafana, or Datadog to monitor training time, artifact volume, and CPU usage during runs

- Automate rollback in case of deployment failure, reverting to the last Production version

- Use conditional logic for technical decisions in the pipeline, based on validated metrics rather than hardcoded values

- Share automation scripts in a separate repository with clear documentation for maintenance and expansion

- Periodically review the pipeline to adapt logic based on project evolution, tooling changes, or business needs

Strategic Summary

Integrating MLflow with CI/CD pipelines transforms it from an experimentation platform into an operational foundation for continuous model delivery. It ensures that every new version is tested, validated, and deployed with traceability, security, and minimal human intervention. Automating the model lifecycle is not just a technical choice — it is a decisive step toward maturity in Machine Learning engineering. By connecting MLflow to the automation flows already used in software, teams can reach real scale with consistency, control, and efficiency. The result is a reliable operation where every production model has passed formal validations, is documented, versioned, and auditable at any point in time. This is how to build a robust, sustainable, and scalable AI delivery pipeline.

CHAPTER 11. METRIC VISUALIZATION AND ANALYSIS

Decision-making in Machine Learning projects must be based on objective and easily interpretable data. A model's success is not defined only by its accuracy or error rate, but by the ability to identify performance nuances, compare versions, understand variations, and justify technical choices. Visualization and metric analysis are the mechanisms that transform experimentation into learning. With MLflow, this process is handled as a native function, allowing metrics to be logged, compared, queried, and visualized in an intuitive and traceable way—via both graphical interface and code.

Every run recorded in MLflow Tracking can contain multiple metrics. These metrics represent model performance indicators for a specific task. The primary metric—such as accuracy, RMSE, or F1—is typically used as a promotion criterion, but secondary metrics are equally important for understanding model stability, balance, and trade-offs.

Metrics are logged during the run using functions like mlflow.log_metric() or automatically via autolog(), which captures values produced by modeling libraries.

python

```
mlflow.log_metric("accuracy", 0.937)

mlflow.log_metric("f1", 0.882)

mlflow.log_metric("precision", 0.905)

mlflow.log_metric("recall", 0.861)
```

These logs ensure that, once the run completes, results are available in MLflow's interface, associated with the run ID and visually organized through interactive graphs. The run comparison screen allows selection of multiple runs and plots their metrics across different axes, making it easier to identify patterns, anomalies, and superior versions.

In addition to final metrics, MLflow allows time-series logging, useful for tracking training progress. This is done by logging multiple log_metric() calls with the same name but different timestamps or steps.

python

```
for epoch in range(1, 11):

    mlflow.log_metric("loss", loss_values[epoch], step=epoch)
```

The corresponding chart will display the loss curve over time, helping identify overfitting, underfitting, or training instability.

These curves can be viewed directly in the web interface with zoom controls, filters, and run comparisons. For example, you can compare the learning curves of two models using different learning rates or regularizations and see which one converges faster or with less fluctuation.

The interface also allows sorting and filtering runs by any registered metric. You can, for example, find all runs with accuracy above 0.9 and training time under 300 seconds. These visual queries are valuable during intense experimentation phases, when dozens or hundreds of runs are executed with minor parameter variations.

Beyond the interface, MLflow offers a robust API for querying, analyzing, and comparing metrics programmatically. This is useful for building automated reports, custom dashboards, or integrating results with other analytical tools.

python

```
from mlflow.tracking import MlflowClient

client = MlflowClient()
runs = client.search_runs(
    experiment_ids=["1"],
    filter_string="metrics.f1 > 0.85 and tags.model='xgboost'",
    order_by=["metrics.f1 DESC"]
)
```

This script returns all runs with F1 scores above 0.85, associated with the XGBoost model, sorted from best to worst. This can feed real-time dashboards, internal version recommendation systems, or deployment automation.

Another strategic use of metric visualization is in **regression testing**. In CI/CD pipelines, you can compare the latest version's metric against the current production version and reject promotion if there's degradation.

python

```
current_version = new_run.data.metrics["f1"]
production_version = production_run.data.metrics["f1"]
if current_version >= production_version:
    promote()
```

This programmatic comparison turns metrics into technical gates, formalizing the validation process and preventing silent regressions.

Besides numerical metrics, MLflow allows saving files such as precision-recall graphs, ROC curves, confusion matrices, or any other visualizations created with libraries like Matplotlib, Seaborn, or Plotly. These files can be saved as artifacts using log_artifact() and are accessible with the run.

python

```
plt.savefig("roc_curve.png")
mlflow.log_artifact("roc_curve.png")
```

These visualizations can be opened directly in MLflow's interface or downloaded via API, serving as visual documentation of model performance and supporting presentations, reports, and validations.

For projects that require custom or interactive visualizations, dashboards can be built by integrating MLflow with libraries like Dash, Streamlit, or Gradio. Metrics can be extracted via API and displayed in real-time with filters, sliders, and responsive charts.

Additionally, MLflow supports grouping runs by tags, which facilitates comparisons by group, scenario, or configuration. A tag such as dataset_version allows grouping all runs using a specific data snapshot, isolating the impact of data changes on model performance.

python

```
mlflow.set_tag("dataset_version", "april-2025")
```

These tags become powerful filters in the visualization interface, enabling cross-analysis of variables like model type, data source, run author, framework used, or any other relevant metadata.

Common Errors and Solutions

Error: "Metric not shown in UI"
Probable Cause: Metric logged outside of the run block or with indentation error.
Recommended Solution: Ensure log_metric() is called within a with mlflow.start_run() block.

Error: "Plot not displayed" when opening artifact
Probable Cause: File saved in an unsupported browser format (e.g., .fig from Matplotlib).
Recommended Solution: Save charts in universal formats like .png, .jpg, or .pdf.

Error: "Metric value overwritten"
Probable Cause: Metric logged multiple times with the same name and no step specified.
Recommended Solution: Use the step= parameter when logging time-series data.

Error: "Filter expression invalid" when querying runs
Probable Cause: Incorrect syntax or non-existent field.
Recommended Solution: Validate the exact metric name and review the filter expression per official documentation.

Error: "Run not found" when accessing metrics via code
Probable Cause: Incorrect run ID or improperly loaded experiment.
Recommended Solution: Confirm the run ID in the UI and ensure the correct experiment is selected.

Best Practices

- Log all relevant task metrics, even those not used as primary evaluation criteria.

- Use composite or derived metrics like f1_macro, gmean, or mcc when balanced evaluation is required.

- Always save learning and loss curves—they help diagnose structural model issues.

- Document metric meanings in artifacts or tags to aid interpretation by team members.

- Avoid obscure abbreviations in metric names—use descriptive, standardized names.

- Use tags to indicate context, like model=xgboost, dataset=april, normalization=zscore, enabling filtered comparisons.

- Centralize metric visualization scripts in a separate module for reuse across experiments.

- Validate data before computing metrics—metrics based on faulty inputs lead to misleading conclusions and poor models.

- Include variance analysis of metrics when evaluating models across different segments or populations.

- Compare models not by a single metric alone, but by a set of criteria—production decisions should weigh robustness, generalization, and efficiency.

Strategic Summary

Metric visualization and analysis is the link that connects experimentation to technical decision-making. Without it, each run would be just an isolated number. With it, patterns emerge, comparisons are made, learning happens, and decisions are justified. MLflow provides a powerful structure for capturing, querying, and interpreting these metrics with clarity, traceability, and fluency. Integrating metric analysis into the Machine Learning workflow ensures that every decision —on parameters, models, or versions—is backed by verifiable, auditable, and reusable data.

CHAPTER 12. FEATURE ENGINEERING AND PREPROCESSING

The effectiveness of a Machine Learning model directly depends on the quality of the variables that feed it. Raw data is rarely ready to be used in modeling algorithms. It requires cleaning, transformation, and reorganization. This stage is known as feature engineering and preprocessing. When poorly executed, it compromises the entire pipeline. When well structured, it defines the model's competitive edge. In the context of MLflow, this stage must not only be effective but also reproducible, traceable, and integrated into the complete cycle of versioning and deployment.

Feature engineering is the process of creating, transforming, and selecting explanatory variables that feed a model. **Preprocessing** is the set of operations applied before actual modeling — from data cleaning to normalization, encoding, outlier handling, and missing value imputation. These processes are essential to ensure statistical consistency, model stability, and generalization capability. In MLflow, the structure of these transformations must be embedded into the pipeline, logged as an artifact, and, when possible, versioned along with the model.

To begin, it's critical to understand the role of features. They carry the information the algorithm uses to make decisions. A noisy, collinear, redundant, or poorly formatted feature can lead the model to learn false patterns, amplify bias, or fail to generalize. Thus, the initial focus must be on ensuring quality without sacrificing useful variability.

The preprocessing pipeline can be built with libraries such as Scikit-learn, Pandas, Feature-engine, or fully customized. A typical pipeline may include:

- Identifying and removing missing values

- Encoding categorical variables

- Normalizing or standardizing scales

- Applying logarithmic or polynomial transformations

- Creating derived (synthetic) variables

- Selecting variables based on importance or correlation

These steps should be built sequentially and deterministically, preferably encapsulated in reusable objects like Scikit-learn's Pipeline.

python

```
from sklearn.pipeline import Pipeline

from sklearn.preprocessing import StandardScaler,
OneHotEncoder

from sklearn.impute import SimpleImputer

from sklearn.compose import ColumnTransformer


num_attributes = ["age", "income"]

cat_attributes = ["marital_status", "profession"]
```

```
num_pipeline = Pipeline([
    ("imputer", SimpleImputer(strategy="median")),
    ("scaler", StandardScaler())
])


cat_pipeline = Pipeline([
    ("imputer", SimpleImputer(strategy="most_frequent")),
    ("onehot", OneHotEncoder(handle_unknown="ignore"))
])


preprocessor = ColumnTransformer([
    ("num", num_pipeline, num_attributes),
    ("cat", cat_pipeline, cat_attributes)
])
```

The preprocessor object can be used to transform the training data and should be saved as part of the final model artifact.

python

```
preprocessor.fit(X_train)
X_train_transformed = preprocessor.transform(X_train)


import mlflow.sklearn
mlflow.sklearn.log_model(preprocessor,
"preprocessing_pipeline")
```

With this registration, any future execution can load the pipeline and apply the exact same transformations—even if the code evolves or the environment changes. This is key to avoiding **training-serving skew**, where the model receives differently transformed data between training and deployment.

Feature engineering also includes creating derived variables. This is where domain expertise meets statistical knowledge. Variables such as ratios, boolean indicators, groupings, conditional counts, or temporal transformations (lags, moving averages, seasonality) can differentiate a generic model from one finely tuned to the real problem.

These features should be created programmatically and logged. Avoid manual or untraceable manipulations. Each transformation function should be encapsulated, documented, and tested—not just for reproducibility but for reusability in other projects.

python

```python
def create_features(df):
    df["income_per_age"] = df["income"] / (df["age"] + 1)
    df["profession_freq"] =
df["profession"].map(df["profession"].value_counts(normalize=
True))
    return df
```

This function can be included as part of the pipeline, and its effects should be audited through distribution logs and descriptive statistics.

Handling missing values is also critical. The imputation strategy must consider the impact on data variance and bias.

Imputing with the mean or median may suffice in some contexts, but in others, adding a flag to indicate the missingness can improve model performance.

python

```
df["income_na"] = df["income"].isna().astype(int)
df["income"] = df["income"].fillna(df["income"].median())
```

This treatment is particularly useful where missing data is informative. MLflow can log these transformations as part of the run's source code or as artifacts.

When working with categorical variables, choosing between OneHotEncoder, LabelEncoder, or techniques like TargetEncoding should depend on data volume, variable cardinality, and the deployment strategy. Target-based encoding, for instance, can provide information gain but requires care to avoid data leakage from test into training sets.

Using OneHotEncoder is suitable for variables with low cardinality:

python

```
from sklearn.preprocessing import OneHotEncoder


encoder = OneHotEncoder(handle_unknown="ignore", sparse_output=False)

X_cat = encoder.fit_transform(df[["marital_status"]])
```

For high-cardinality variables or datasets with high dimensionality, ordinal encoding or rare category grouping may be better suited.

Normalization of numerical data is another key consideration.

Distance- or gradient-based models—like SVMs, neural networks, or logistic regression—benefit from features on comparable scales. Use StandardScaler or MinMaxScaler with fit on the training set and transform on future data to ensure scale parameters aren't influenced by unseen data.

Feature engineering must always be built as part of the complete pipeline—from ingestion to deployment. This prevents disconnected transformations and ensures that the model is always fed data in the same format and structure as during training. In MLflow, this means logging the full pipeline as a single artifact or embedding it as a preprocessor in log_model().

python

```
from sklearn.pipeline import Pipeline

from sklearn.linear_model import LogisticRegression


full_model = Pipeline([

    ("preprocessing", preprocessor),

    ("classifier", LogisticRegression())

])


full_model.fit(X_train, y_train)


mlflow.sklearn.log_model(full_model, "pipeline_model")
```

This model encapsulates all transformations and the prediction algorithm, creating a unified, traceable object ready for deployment. It is the safest way to prevent environment inconsistencies.

Common Errors and Solutions

Error: "ValueError: input contains NaN"
Probable Cause: Input data was not processed through the imputation pipeline.
Recommended Solution: Ensure the preprocessing pipeline is applied to all data before fit or predict.

Error: "Found unknown categories during transform"
Probable Cause: OneHotEncoder received a new category not seen during training.
Recommended Solution: Set handle_unknown="ignore" or use rare category grouping strategies.

Error: "Feature mismatch between training and inference"
Probable Cause: Difference in number/order of features between training and deployment.
Recommended Solution: Encapsulate all transformations into a pipeline and save it with the model using MLflow.

Error: "NotFittedError: This transformer instance is not fitted yet"
Probable Cause: Calling transform() without executing fit().
Recommended Solution: Ensure correct function call order and confirm fitting was performed.

Error: "KeyError" when accessing transformed column
Probable Cause: Column name changed or original variable was deleted.
Recommended Solution: Maintain consistent column naming and document transformations.

Best Practices

- Encapsulate all transformations in reusable, well-documented pipelines

- Log pipelines as artifacts using mlflow.sklearn.log_model() to ensure traceability

- Use standardized naming for steps and columns to simplify readability and maintenance

- Validate transformed feature distributions with plots and descriptive statistics

- Perform feature importance analysis to remove irrelevant or noisy variables

- Include domain-specific transformations, even simple ones—they add informative value

- Test transformation robustness with out-of-sample data simulating production conditions

- Avoid future data dependencies or target leakage in preprocessing

- Evaluate each transformation's impact on the model's main metric

- Keep detailed logs of each step to simplify audit and reproduction

Strategic Summary

Feature engineering and preprocessing are the technical pillars on which robust models are built. In the context of MLflow, these stages must not be treated as preliminary or auxiliary, but as central parts of the experimentation and delivery pipeline.

Transformations must be traceable, versioned, and integrated into the final model. By mastering this process, teams improve the accuracy, reliability, and scalability of their solutions. More than transforming data, this is where business knowledge becomes useful variables—and useful variables become models that generate real impact.

.

CHAPTER 13. SECURITY AND ACCESS CONTROL

Machine Learning projects don't just handle data and algorithms —they operate within organizational contexts that demand compliance, information protection, and action traceability. As experimentation workflows mature and models reach production, the need to establish clear security and access control policies becomes increasingly critical. MLflow, as an operational platform for the model lifecycle, must be deployed with these principles in mind. This involves defining permissions for experiments, controlling model changes, authenticating users, isolating environments, and protecting sensitive artifacts.

Security in ML projects should not be treated as an add-on. It must be built into the architecture from the start. This means defining who can train, register, promote, deploy, and delete models—and ensuring every action is traceable. It also means protecting the data used in experiments, validating the executed code, and controlling access to the underlying compute resources.

In the MLflow context, the basic security structure can be organized into three complementary layers:

- **Access to the tracking server**

- **Artifact protection**

- **Control over Model Registry operations**

Each layer should be governed by distinct policies and, where possible, integrated into the organization's identity system.

The first step is ensuring that the MLflow Tracking Server is only accessible to authorized users. By default, MLflow has no authentication—anyone with access to the port can register experiments, view metrics, and retrieve artifacts. This is unacceptable in professional environments. The server must be protected using a reverse proxy with basic authentication, OAuth2, SSO (Single Sign-On), or integrations with systems like Keycloak or Azure AD.

One of the simplest protection methods is using **NGINX with basic authentication**:

nginx

```
server {
    listen 443 ssl;
    server_name mlflow.domain.com;

    ssl_certificate /etc/nginx/ssl/cert.pem;
    ssl_certificate_key /etc/nginx/ssl/key.pem;

    location / {
        proxy_pass http://localhost:5000;
        auth_basic "Restricted Area";
        auth_basic_user_file /etc/nginx/.htpasswd;
    }
}
```

This prevents unauthenticated users from accessing the web UI or REST API. It can be replaced with token-based authentication or OAuth2 depending on your infrastructure.

The **second layer** is **artifact protection**. When experiments are logged, artifacts—models, images, logs, and transformations—are saved in a storage backend. This may be a local directory or a cloud service like Amazon S3, Azure Blob Storage, or Google Cloud Storage. Security here depends on two factors: **where** the artifacts are stored, and **who** has access.

If using cloud storage, it's recommended to use **temporary credentials** with **scoped access**. For example, in AWS S3, policies can be configured to allow read-only access to production artifacts and write access only for authenticated pipelines.

Minimal policy for artifact read access:

- Access to a specific bucket and prefix only

- No delete permissions

- No global listing permission

Additionally, enable encryption at rest and in transit. Artifacts should be transmitted via HTTPS and stored encrypted with organization-managed KMS keys.

The **third layer** is **control over the Model Registry**, which is the most sensitive component, defining which models are in production, in validation, or deprecated. Allowing any user to alter model stages undermines the entire governance process. Access to the Registry must be tightly controlled.

While MLflow does not natively support **RBAC (role-based access control)**, this can be implemented around the server via an API Gateway or internal wrappers. The safest pattern is to create an intermediate API that receives stage transition commands and authenticates whether the user is authorized.

Typical control scenario:

- **Data scientists** can register models and promote to *Staging*

- **MLOps engineers** can promote to *Production*

- **Administrators** can delete models or versions

This control can be orchestrated through automation scripts that validate identity tokens or via external identity management services (e.g., federated identity providers).

Another good practice is to **log the author of every run and stage transition** as a tag or description in the Registry. This doesn't prevent misuse, but ensures actions can be audited later.

python

```
client.set_tag(run_id, "executed_by", "joao.silva")

client.update_model_version(name="model_x", version="2",
description="promoted by j.silva after staging validation")
```

This detailed logging creates an **auditable technical trail**, essential in regulated projects or environments with multiple stakeholders.

Beyond these three main layers, consider the following security practices:

- **Environment isolation** – prevent experiment code from accessing production infrastructure

- **Resource limits** – enforce quotas for CPU, memory, and disk usage

- **Code validation** – use linters, unit tests, and security scanners on submitted code

- **Mandatory versioning** – require model deployments to be linked to a specific code commit

- **Periodic backups** – back up databases and artifacts regularly, with integrity checks

Common Errors and Solutions

Error: "Access denied to artifact store"
Probable Cause: The server's credentials don't have permissions on the storage bucket or directory.
Recommended Solution: Create a restricted but sufficient access policy, and test with authenticated clients.

Error: "Unauthorized model transition"
Probable Cause: Attempt to change a model's stage without authentication or with limited permissions.
Recommended Solution: Implement an authorization layer or separate staging/production control via credentials.

Error: "Insecure content loaded over HTTP"
Probable Cause: MLflow interface served over HTTP instead of HTTPS.
Recommended Solution: Use NGINX or another proxy with SSL/TLS enabled, and redirect HTTP to HTTPS.

Error: "Run owner unknown"
Probable Cause: Run logged without authentication or author tag.
Recommended Solution: Require metadata at run creation and authenticated tokens for any submissions.

Error: "Model version overwritten"
Probable Cause: Manual model registration with same name and

no version control.

Recommended Solution: Automate versioning with increment logic and restrict manual overwrites through permissions.

Best Practices

- Always expose the MLflow server behind an authenticated, HTTPS-enabled proxy

- Define access control policies based on roles—even if implemented manually

- Secure buckets and storage using identity-based authentication instead of shared access keys

- Log author, purpose, and justification for each model transition in the Registry

- Regularly audit access logs to review user activity and model changes

- Automate security tests in the pipeline, including dependency analysis and vulnerability scans

- Use short-lived tokens for CI/CD and automated jobs

- Configure alerts for critical actions like model deletion, promotion to production, and authentication failures

- Isolate *Staging* and *Production* environments on separate infrastructure with distinct permissions

- Establish a formal model governance policy defining who can do what based on risk and responsibility

Strategic Summary

Security and access control in Machine Learning projects are not optional—they are foundational elements of operational maturity. As models become strategic assets impacting real-world processes and decisions, demands for traceability, version control, permission management, and protection from unauthorized changes increase. MLflow provides the infrastructure to track actions, log authorship, and version models—but its real effectiveness depends on the implementation of complementary policies and strong security practices. Embedding these from the beginning ensures that the growth of AI operations doesn't come with structural vulnerabilities. Security is not something added at the end— it is the trust foundation on which production-ready Machine Learning solutions are built.

CHAPTER 14. STORAGE SCALABILITY

As Machine Learning projects grow in maturity, volume, and collaboration, the ability to efficiently store data, artifacts, models, and logs evolves from an operational detail into a strategic requirement. The volume of technical artifacts generated by repeated runs, model versions, metric logs, and parallel storage can compromise system performance and user experience if not addressed with a scalable storage architecture. MLflow, by default, supports multiple backend types for metadata and artifact storage. However, scaling these layers responsibly requires a structured and predictable approach.

Storage scalability in MLflow is directly tied to the separation of two essential components:

- **Backend Store**: Responsible for experiment metadata, such as parameters, metrics, run IDs, model names, and registry stages

- **Artifact Store**: Responsible for physical files generated by each run, such as models, plots, reports, and transformations

The backend typically uses a relational database (SQLite, PostgreSQL, MySQL), while the artifact store may reside in local file systems, cloud buckets (Amazon S3, Azure Blob, GCS), or mounted network volumes (NFS, EFS). The choice for these layers should factor in access concurrency, latency, fault tolerance, and replication ease.

Starting with the backend, using SQLite in production is highly discouraged. It's designed for low-concurrency write environments and cannot support multiple simultaneous connections with reliable performance. In professional environments, the minimum standard is PostgreSQL or MySQL with connection pooling, read replication, and continuous backup.

Backend migration is straightforward—simply change the connection URI:

bash

```
mlflow server \
  --backend-store-uri postgresql://user:password@host:port/mlflow \
  --default-artifact-root s3://bucket_mlflow/ \
  --host 0.0.0.0 \
  --port 5000
```

On the artifact store side, data volume grows quickly. Each run may generate dozens or hundreds of files, and often experiments are duplicated with minimal changes. The key strategy is separating **hot storage** (frequently accessed data) from **cold storage** (archived or historical data). Buckets with versioning enabled, lifecycle policies, and automatic compression are essential to keeping costs under control.

Amazon S3, for example, supports lifecycle policies that:

- Move artifacts older than 30 days to Infrequent Access (IA) storage

- Archive objects older than 90 days in Glacier Deep Archive

- Automatically delete files after X days without access

These policies can be configured directly in the bucket console using conditional rules by prefix (e.g., /runs/, /models/, /historical_artifacts).

Another strategy is **artifact deduplication**. In many projects, the same models or files are saved multiple times. Tools like DVC, LakeFS, or content-addressed file systems can be integrated into the pipeline to detect duplicates and save real storage space.

It's also possible to implement **automatic file compression** before sending to the artifact store:

python

```
import zipfile


with zipfile.ZipFile("full_model.zip", "w") as zipf:
    zipf.write("model.pkl")
    zipf.write("pipeline.pkl")


mlflow.log_artifact("full_model.zip")
```

This practice significantly reduces storage volume—especially useful for runs with many files or large logs.

A critical point is **managing obsolete versions**. Without a clear policy, the Registry can accumulate hundreds of outdated models. Ideally, automate the archiving of versions that:

- Are not in *Production* or *Staging*

- Were created more than six months ago

- Do not have a recurrent usage tag

This can be done using MLflow's API:

python

```
from mlflow.tracking import MlflowClient

client = MlflowClient()
versions = client.search_model_versions("name='credit_model'")
for v in versions:
    if v.current_stage == "None" and int(v.creation_timestamp) < cutoff_timestamp:
        client.transition_model_version_stage(v.name, v.version, stage="Archived")
```

This kind of automation reduces storage usage and keeps the Registry clean and queryable, focused only on relevant versions.

In addition to MLflow's own data, experiments often rely on large datasets, stored locally or in external buckets. Scalability here must consider local caching, file chunking, compact binary formats (like Parquet or Feather), and parallel reading. Libraries like Dask, Vaex, or Spark can partition data and process it in parallel.

For datasets hosted in S3, avoid many small requests and prefer batch reads using prefix filters and adjusted page sizes. The same goes for execution logs, which should be sent in blocks and processed by dedicated observability tools (such as ELK, Loki, Datadog, or Prometheus), instead of relying solely on the artifact store.

Architecturally, a mature storage scalability strategy should include:

- Artifacts stored in versioned buckets with archiving policies

- Metadata backend with replication and automatic backup

- Compression and deduplication of artifacts

- Scheduled cleanup and archiving routines

- Separation of environments (dev, staging, production) with distinct storage

- Operational logs and metrics stored outside MLflow in specialized systems

- Asynchronous pipelines for large file uploads or heavy results

Common Errors and Solutions

Error: "Too many open files"
Probable Cause: Pipeline trying to open dozens of artifacts simultaneously.
Recommended Solution: Use context managers (with open) and limit concurrency via IO pools or control mechanisms.

Error: "Request time out writing artifact"
Probable Cause: High latency during uploads to cloud buckets.
Recommended Solution: Enable pre-upload compression and use asynchronous sending with progressive retries.

Error: "Database lock timeout"
Probable Cause: Underpowered relational backend or lack of

connection pooling.
Recommended Solution: Use connection pools and scalable DBs like PostgreSQL with read replicas.

Error: "Artifact not found" when accessing old run
Probable Cause: Object was moved to cold storage without direct read permissions.
Recommended Solution: Set automatic restore policies or migrate critical artifacts to high-availability buckets.

Error: "Storage quota exceeded"
Probable Cause: Uncontrolled file growth in duplicate or test runs.
Recommended Solution: Implement version control, compression, and automatic retention policies.

Best Practices

- Use scalable buckets like S3, Azure Blob, or GCS with versioning enabled

- Configure automated lifecycle policies for archiving, compressing, and deleting old artifacts

- Use dedicated relational DBs with backup, replication, and continuous monitoring for the backend

- Automate cleanup, deduplication, and archiving scripts using technical metadata

- Divide artifact storage into hot (active), warm (queryable), and cold (backup) tiers

- Avoid many small files—prefer single files with internal structure (e.g., ZIP, TAR, HDF5)

- Document file organization schemas and directory prefixes for easier queries and maintenance

- Integrate volume monitoring with alerts to anticipate quota overruns

- Periodically clean non-productive runs such as local tests, temporary validations, or invalid experiments

- Forecast storage budget and simulate growth based on run frequency, artifact volume, and retention duration

Strategic Summary

Storage scalability is a core competency in operating Machine Learning projects at scale. MLflow provides the framework for logging and versioning artifacts, but its effectiveness depends on architectural decisions that ensure persistence, access speed, resilience, and cost control. Projects that ignore this aspect often collapse under their own data. Meanwhile, those that plan for scalability can support hundreds of models, thousands of runs, and continuous experimentation cycles with stability and confidence. Good storage isn't just about keeping data—it's about knowing how to retrieve, maintain, scale, and evolve it. This is the technical foundation for durable and efficient ML operations.

CHAPTER 15. INTEGRATION WITH CLOUD PROVIDERS

Efficient execution of Machine Learning projects requires elastic infrastructure, scalable storage, distributed processing, and continuous delivery mechanisms. These needs naturally converge with the features offered by major cloud providers such as Amazon Web Services (AWS), Microsoft Azure, and Google Cloud Platform (GCP). Integrating MLflow with these environments is a critical step to ensure models can be trained, monitored, versioned, and deployed at scale—with security, traceability, and optimized resource usage. This integration should not be treated as a post-hoc adjustment, but rather as a native component of the model lifecycle architecture.

MLflow offers flexible support for cloud-based execution. Its components—Tracking Server, Artifact Store, Backend Store, Model Registry, and APIs—can be hosted, distributed, and consumed across any infrastructure compatible with standard HTTP protocols, relational databases, and cloud storage systems. The key to successful integration lies in orchestration of resources, permission control, and standardized endpoints.

The first architectural decision is where the Tracking Server will be hosted. It can run on an EC2 instance (AWS), a VM in Compute Engine (GCP), an Azure VM, or as a container in Kubernetes. What matters is that it is reachable via HTTPS, protected by authentication, and authorized to write to the configured backend and artifact services.

For production environments, the best practice is to run the

MLflow Tracking Server in a **Docker container** orchestrated by services like ECS (AWS), AKS (Azure), or GKE (Google), with integration to load balancers and managed SSL certificates.

bash

```
docker run -d \
  -p 5000:5000 \
  -e BACKEND_STORE_URI=postgresql://user:password@host/db \
  -e ARTIFACT_ROOT=s3://bucket-mlflow \
  -v ~/.aws:/root/.aws \
  mlflow/mlflow:latest \
  mlflow server \
  --backend-store-uri $BACKEND_STORE_URI \
  --default-artifact-root $ARTIFACT_ROOT \
  --host 0.0.0.0 \
  --port 5000
```

This container can be configured with network security policies, auto-scaling, and centralized monitoring.

The **backend store** can be hosted in services like RDS (AWS), Cloud SQL (GCP), or Azure Database for PostgreSQL. It should be configured with automatic backups, encryption, and security group access rules.

The **artifact store** typically uses object buckets, configured with regional settings, versioning enabled, encryption at rest (SSE or CMK), and lifecycle policies for cost optimization.

Amazon S3:

- Enable versioning with aws s3api put-bucket-versioning

- Define lifecycle policies to move old objects to Infrequent Access or Glacier

- Control access via IAM Roles or policies attached to EC2 or Lambda

Azure Blob:

- Create containers with geographic redundancy

- Use SAS tokens with expiration for temporary access

- Configure automatic retention and archiving rules

Google Cloud Storage:

- Enable **Uniform Bucket-Level Access**

- Create policies using IAM roles (Storage Object Viewer, Storage Object Creator)

- Use CMEK (Customer Managed Encryption Keys) for compliance when needed

To allow MLflow to interact with these storages, the container or instance must have appropriate credentials. In AWS, this is done using an **IAM Role** attached to the instance. In GCP, with a **Service Account** attached to the VM or Pod. In Azure, via **Managed Identity** or SAS token usage.

Beyond storage, **model deployment** can be done directly on cloud platforms. MLflow supports exporting models to be served as APIs in:

- **Amazon SageMaker**, via mlflow.sagemaker.deploy()

- **Azure ML**, using azureml-mlflow integration

- **GCP AI Platform**, exporting in compatible format and deploying via SDK

AWS SageMaker:

python

```
import mlflow.sagemaker

mlflow.sagemaker.deploy(
    model_uri="models:/CreditClassifier/Production",
    region_name="us-east-1",
    mode="replace",
    execution_role_arn="arn:aws:iam::123456789012:role/SageMakerExecutionRole",
    instance_type="ml.m5.large",
    instance_count=1,
    app_name="credit-classifier-endpoint"
)
```

The model becomes available as a REST API, with token-based authentication and integration with CloudWatch for monitoring.

In **Azure**, deployment can be done with azureml.core and embedded MLflow. The model is registered and published as an inference service with autoscaling and traffic routing.

In **GCP**, the exported model is uploaded to **AI Platform** using gcloud ai models upload and configured with synchronous or asynchronous prediction endpoints.

Additionally, the cloud enables scaling model training using GPU instances, Spark clusters, serverless services, and orchestrated pipelines with **Airflow**, **Vertex AI Pipelines**, or **Azure ML Pipelines**.

MLflow Projects can be used in these pipelines to run standardized tasks with parameterized inputs and isolated environments:

bash

```
mlflow run https://github.com/org/mlflow-project -P
learning_rate=0.01 -P n_estimators=100
```

This command can be included as an automated step within more complex workflows.

A critical integration point is **secret management**. Variables such as DB URIs, API tokens, and access keys must **not** be stored in source code. Instead, they should be protected in services like:

- **AWS Secrets Manager**

- **Azure Key Vault**

- **GCP Secret Manager**

These secrets should be accessed at runtime using application-based identity authentication, reducing leak risks and enabling centralized revocation.

Cloud integration should also include **observability**. MLflow logs and metrics should be routed to:

- **CloudWatch Logs** (AWS)

- **Azure Monitor / Log Analytics**

- **Google Cloud Logging**

This allows monitoring of execution time, artifact volume, deployment failures, call volume, and critical events.

For **multicloud or hybrid environments**, isolate environments by prefix or project and maintain modular backend and storage configurations. MLflow supports multiple instances and enables separation by experiment, business line, or geographic region.

Common Errors and Solutions

Error: "Permission denied when uploading artifact"
Probable Cause: IAM Role or Service Account lacks write access to the bucket.
Recommended Solution: Review access policy and ensure the role includes s3:PutObject, storage.objects.create, or equivalent.

Error: "Endpoint not found" after SageMaker deployment
Probable Cause: App name mismatch or versioning conflict.
Recommended Solution: Check app and model names, and validate endpoint conflicts.

Error: "No module named azureml"
Probable Cause: Azure ML SDK not installed in the environment.
Recommended Solution: Add azureml-core and azureml-mlflow to the Conda environment or container.

Error: "Secret not found" accessing Key Vault or Secrets Manager
Probable Cause: Application lacks access permission to the secret store.
Recommended Solution: Ensure the application's identity has secret reader permissions.

Error: "Bucket location constraint error"
Probable Cause: Region mismatch between bucket, instance, or service.

Recommended Solution: Align regions across bucket, instance, and services to avoid replication conflicts.

Best Practices

- Use dedicated buckets for MLflow with versioning and lifecycle policies

- Protect URIs, keys, and tokens in the cloud's secret managers

- Run the Tracking Server in a container with authentication and SSL, using a cloud load balancer

- Separate environments by project with distinct backend and artifact stores

- Use Service Accounts, IAM Roles, and Managed Identities to securely control permissions

- Automate deployments with direct MLflow integration to cloud inference platforms

- Configure alerts for deployment failures, storage usage, and unusual execution volumes

- Automate metadata DB backups and replicate critical buckets across availability zones

- Maintain centralized logs with search, filters, and at least 30-day retention

- Forecast cloud budget based on run frequency, average artifact size, and inference load

Strategic Summary

Integrating MLflow with cloud providers is the decisive step to transform local experiments into distributed, auditable, and scalable operations. By connecting tracking, storage, deployment, and governance to cloud infrastructure, ML teams gain elasticity, security, and control. The goal isn't just to move MLflow to the cloud—it's to make the cloud the operational backbone for continuous modeling and delivery cycles. The cloud shifts from a technical utility to a competitive advantage. Teams that structure this integration well build resilient, observable, production-ready pipelines with full governance and the ability to scale with business growth.

CHAPTER 16. PRODUCTION MODEL DEPLOYMENT

Machine Learning models do not generate value while merely stored in directories or logged in experiments. Real impact occurs when these models are effectively put into operation, receiving real-world data and returning predictions with reliability, security, and performance. This transition from experimental to production environments is called *deployment*. In the MLflow context, model deployment is a critical stage that must be architected with precision, traceability, and adherence to engineering best practices. It's the point where technical operations meet the end user, the digital product, or the automated system consuming algorithmic decisions.

MLflow offers multiple ways to operationalize registered models —from local REST endpoints to direct integrations with managed services such as Amazon SageMaker, Azure ML, or Kubernetes. The central goal is to ensure that any model available in the Model Registry can be securely invoked, monitored in real time, scaled with demand, and quickly reverted in case of failure.

The most direct way to deploy a registered MLflow model is using the mlflow models serve command. This launches a local prediction server exposing a REST API with standardized endpoints for data input and prediction output.

bash

```
mlflow models serve -m models:/CreditClassifier/Production -p 5000 --no-conda
```

This server can be placed behind a reverse proxy (like NGINX), with authentication and HTTPS support, and integrated with load balancers such as AWS ALB or Google Cloud Load Balancer.

By default, the /invocations endpoint receives a JSON payload like:

json

```
{
  "columns": ["age", "income", "marital_status"],
  "data": [[32, 4500, "single"]]
}
```

And returns an array of predictions:

json

```
[0.91]
```

Local deployment is useful for testing, prototyping, model validation, and integration with internal systems. However, for real production environments, the recommendation is to **package the server into a Docker container**, preloaded with the model and environment, and orchestrate it on managed clusters.

MLflow allows Docker image creation with the embedded model using build-docker:

bash

```
mlflow models build-docker -m models:/CreditClassifier/Production -n mlflow-credit-classifier:latest
```

This image can be published to repositories like Amazon ECR, Docker Hub, or Azure Container Registry, and deployed on services such as ECS, AKS, GKE, or on-premises.

For infrastructures already consolidated in managed services, deployment can be done directly via SDK. A native integration example is with **Amazon SageMaker**:

python

```
import mlflow.sagemaker


mlflow.sagemaker.deploy(
    model_uri="models:/CreditClassifier/Production",
    region_name="us-east-1",
    mode="replace",
    execution_role_arn="arn:aws:iam::123456789012:role/SageMakerExecutionRole",
    instance_type="ml.m5.large",
    instance_count=1,
    app_name="credit-classifier-endpoint"
)
```

The model becomes available as a scalable API, with CloudWatch monitoring, IAM-based authentication, and traffic routing for A/B testing.

In **Azure**, deployment is handled via the azureml SDK integrated with MLflow through azureml-mlflow. The process involves registering the model, creating a Docker image, configuring the inference environment, and publishing the endpoint.

In **Google Cloud**, deployment is managed via **Vertex AI**, with the model exported from MLflow in a compatible format (e.g., SavedModel, ONNX, pickle) and configured with versioning, OAuth2 authentication, and autoscaling.

Besides direct deployment, **custom servers** can also be configured, including:

- Custom APIs in Flask, FastAPI, or Django

- Compiled language servers with bindings to serialized models

- Lambda Functions for on-demand predictions

- Asynchronous services with messaging queues (Kafka, Pub/Sub, RabbitMQ)

In every scenario, the deployed model must be:

- **Versioned**, with traceable origin in the Model Registry

- **Protected**, with authentication and input validation

- **Monitored**, with usage metrics and error alerts

- **Revertible**, with an automated rollback strategy

Another essential aspect is **data preparation in production**. The preprocessing pipeline used in training must be encapsulated with the model to ensure that incoming API data is transformed identically. This avoids silent errors from feature drift or data mismatch.

python

```
from sklearn.pipeline import Pipeline
```

```
from sklearn.preprocessing import StandardScaler
from sklearn.linear_model import LogisticRegression

pipeline = Pipeline([
    ("scaler", StandardScaler()),
    ("classifier", LogisticRegression())
])

pipeline.fit(X_train, y_train)

mlflow.sklearn.log_model(pipeline, "production_model")
```

This pipeline is saved as a single artifact with embedded transformations. Upon deployment, it performs the same steps without manual reconfiguration.

It's also possible to version the preprocessing pipeline separately and chain it with the final model using a custom wrapper—ideal in environments where transformation logic changes more frequently than modeling.

Post-deployment validation must be routine. This includes:

- Functional tests (known payloads)

- Semantic validation (reasonable outputs for given inputs)

- Performance checks (latency, resource consumption)

Production metrics capture should be automated, including:

- Requests per minute

- HTTP error rate

- Prediction distribution

- Timeout rate

- Anomalous payload logs

These should integrate with observability systems such as **Prometheus**, **Datadog**, **Azure Monitor**, or **CloudWatch**. While MLflow doesn't natively provide this, containerized deployment allows instrumentation via sidecar agents or log agents.

Deployment security must include:

- Authentication (API Key, OAuth2, JWT)

- Rate limiting

- Input schema validation

- Encrypted data in transit

Using an API Gateway helps encapsulate these protections, offering delegated authentication, IP filtering, and billing or quota integration.

Common Errors and Solutions

Error: "ValueError: input shape mismatch"
Probable Cause: Input does not match expected pipeline structure.
Recommended Solution: Validate schema using tools like pydantic or cerberus, and standardize preprocessing.

Error: "404 Not Found" calling endpoint
Probable Cause: Incomplete deployment, incorrect name, or endpoint still provisioning.
Recommended Solution: Check service status, provision time, and model name.

Error: "Permission denied on deploy"
Probable Cause: Credential lacks deploy permissions.
Recommended Solution: Review IAM Role or Service Account permissions and link to the correct project.

Error: "ModuleNotFoundError" during model serving
Probable Cause: Missing dependency in production environment.
Recommended Solution: Ensure deployment environment matches conda.yaml used during training.

Error: "Timeout during prediction"
Probable Cause: Heavy model or costly preprocessing.
Recommended Solution: Optimize pipeline, reduce payload size, or scale infrastructure.

Best Practices

- Package model and preprocessor in a single pipeline for consistency

- Publish versioned endpoint with automatic rollback and version isolation

- Instrument service with configurable logs, metrics, and alerts

- Document endpoints with OpenAPI, including sample payloads and responses

- Use load balancing and replication for fault tolerance and horizontal scaling

- Configure autoscaling based on real load or custom metrics

- Monitor average latency, 95th percentile, and error rate per route

- Use blue/green or canary deployment strategies for safe rollout

- Validate in staging before promoting to production

- Maintain a unique version per production model for audit and troubleshooting

Strategic Summary

Model deployment is where Machine Learning engineering meets business value. A well-trained model that never reaches production is merely an incomplete proof of concept. MLflow provides the tools necessary to make this transition structured, traceable, and sustainable. Integrating models with APIs, monitoring, version control, and security policies turns experimental code into an operational asset. Success lies not just in serving predictions, but in doing so with confidence, speed, and clarity. Deployment is not the end—it's the launch point for continuous learning in production.

CHAPTER 17. MONITORING AND POST-DEPLOYMENT

The lifecycle of a Machine Learning model does not end with deployment. On the contrary, it is only after deployment that the model begins to be tested under real conditions— processing production data, interacting with systems and users, and generating practical impact. At this point, monitoring becomes a technical cornerstone. Monitoring ensures that the model operates stably, responds accurately, handles new data patterns, and maintains statistical integrity. While MLflow is not a monitoring system in itself, it can be integrated with other tools to provide traceability and context, while the surrounding environment delivers the necessary instrumentation for both technical and strategic oversight.

Post-deployment encompasses all actions intended to track model behavior in production, identify deviations, respond to failures, update versions, collect feedback, and generate continuous learning. It is a phase of vigilance and refinement, where the focus shifts from algorithmic performance to operational behavior in complex and dynamic environments.

Model monitoring can be divided into five main axes:

- **Availability**: Is the model reachable and responding as expected?

- **Performance**: Response time, throughput, CPU/memory usage

- **Prediction Quality**: Maintenance of accuracy, recall, F1, or other target metrics

- **Data Stability**: Monitoring for data drift and concept drift

- **Technical Integrity**: Code failures, input errors, artifact degradation

Infrastructure and Instrumentation

The first step in setting up monitoring is ensuring that the inference endpoint or service is instrumented to generate **real-time logs and metrics**. This can be achieved using tools like prometheus_client (Python), agents like Fluent Bit, sidecars like Envoy, or native cloud service APIs.

For **availability and performance**, standard metrics include:

- Requests per minute

- Average response time (latency)

- Latency percentiles (p95, p99)

- HTTP error rates (400s, 500s)

- Timeout rate

- Schema validation rejection rate

These metrics should be exported to tools such as Prometheus, Grafana, Datadog, Azure Monitor, or CloudWatch. For mlflow models serve, it's ideal to use a reverse proxy like NGINX to capture detailed logs and metrics.

Prediction Quality

Monitoring prediction quality requires logging model outputs and, whenever possible, comparing with ground truth once it becomes available. This comparison may occur via sampling or asynchronous pipelines with validation delays.

python

```
log = {
    "input": input_json,
    "output": model.predict(input),
    "timestamp": datetime.utcnow(),
    "model_version": "v4.2"
}
store_inference_log(log)
```

These logs must be versioned, encrypted, and anonymized to comply with regulations like **LGPD** or **GDPR**. With this data, post-production accuracy reports can be generated and compared with offline validation metrics.

Drift Detection

Data drift monitoring involves detecting significant changes in input distributions compared to training data. Tools for this include:

- **EvidentlyAI**

- **Alibi Detect**

- **WhyLogs**

- **Scikit-multiflow**

These libraries calculate distribution statistics (mean, standard deviation, histograms) and divergences (KL Divergence, PSI, Hellinger Distance).

python

```
from evidently.metrics import ColumnDriftMetric
from evidently.report import Report


report =
Report(metrics=[ColumnDriftMetric(column_name="age")])
report.run(reference_data=train_df, current_data=prod_df)
report.save_html("drift_report.html")
```

Such analyses should run periodically (daily, weekly, or by volume) and trigger alerts when thresholds are exceeded.

Concept drift, on the other hand, occurs when the relationship between inputs and target changes. It's harder to detect because it requires comparison between predictions and ground truth over time. A practical approach is monitoring accuracy trends by segment (user groups, regions, etc.).

Traceability and Versioning

In production, it's vital to log the **model version**, input data, score, and final output. This enables not only performance monitoring but also **auditing**.

MLflow supports storing this context as **tags and artifacts** associated with the registered model:

python

```
mlflow.log_artifact("prod_validation_sample.csv",
artifact_path="prod_val")
```

```
mlflow.set_tag("val_date", "2025-03-10")
```

These records allow reconstitution of the context in which a model was validated or rejected.

The **Model Registry** should control version transitions based on live performance metrics. If a model shows significant regression, it can be automatically demoted or replaced:

python

```
if prod_accuracy < min_threshold:

    client.transition_model_version_stage("CreditClassifier",
version="5", stage="Archived")

    client.transition_model_version_stage("CreditClassifier",
version="4", stage="Production")
```

This ensures production always runs the **best proven version**, not just the latest trained.

Feedback Collection

Post-deployment also includes collecting **user feedback**. Whether explicit (confirming/correcting predictions) or implicit (clicks, purchases, conversions), feedback must be logged and linked to the input and model version to enable contextual learning and retraining.

This can be achieved via:

- Event systems (Kafka, Pub/Sub)

- REST APIs

- Database records

- Queueing systems

Execution Environment Monitoring

Finally, monitoring the runtime environment is critical. This includes:

- Infrastructure availability (CPU, memory, disk)

- Active container count

- Average restart times

- Incidents by region

- Cumulative inference costs

These should be integrated into **technical dashboards** and monitored by **SREs** or **ML Ops squads**. Model deployment is part of the system architecture, and its performance directly influences end-user experience.

Common Errors and Solutions

Error: "Predictions are inconsistent across runs"
Cause: Model updated without fixed version or inconsistent pipeline
Recommended Solution: Always log model version, pipeline version, and input parameters

Error: "Drift not detected until severe performance loss"
Cause: No proactive monitoring on input distributions
Recommended Solution: Implement periodic drift checks and automatic alerts

Error: "Timeouts under heavy load"
Cause: Insufficient infrastructure or no autoscaling

Recommended Solution: Adjust replicas, CPU/memory limits, and configure autoscaling

Error: "Metrics inconsistent between train and production"
Cause: Different preprocessing in training vs. production
Recommended Solution: Ensure identical and versioned preprocessing pipelines

Error: "Predictions logged without user feedback"
Cause: No feedback collection or ground truth linkage
Recommended Solution: Establish processes for capturing and linking user feedback

Best Practices

- Implement structured logging: model version, input, output, metadata

- Automate metric calculation from auditable production samples

- Continuously monitor data and concept drift with dedicated tools

- Use revalidation pipelines for every model promoted to production

- Integrate degradation alerts with incident systems (PagerDuty, Slack, Opsgenie)

- Define SLOs (Service Level Objectives) for inference services

- Plan and trigger retraining based on real feedback windows

- Audit historical versions to detect silent errors

- Build stakeholder-facing dashboards (technical and business)

- Document all post-deployment processes as part of model lifecycle governance

Strategic Summary

Monitoring is operating with awareness. It transforms ML models from static code into living components of a critical architecture. Post-deployment requires the same rigor as model development because it is here that a model proves itself useful —or reveals its fragility. MLflow supports tracking, versioning, and logging, but monitoring ensures the journey stays on course. Unmonitored models are black boxes in production. Monitored models are intelligent systems that learn, evolve, and remain aligned with business needs. Monitoring is care. It is the engineering of trust.

CHAPTER 18. USE CASES IN LARGE-SCALE ENVIRONMENTS

Machine Learning projects operating at large scale face challenges that go far beyond what is seen in local or prototypical contexts. Technical complexity increases exponentially with the growth of data volume, diversity of teams, number of models in production, demand for reproducibility, and the need for distributed governance. In this scenario, MLflow emerges as a strategic solution capable of organizing, standardizing, and scaling the model lifecycle. This chapter offers an applied view of how large organizations integrate MLflow into their workflows, highlighting technical patterns, operational pitfalls, and solutions adopted to support robust and auditable AI operations.

In large-scale environments, MLflow is typically used across three simultaneous fronts:

orchestration of multiple teams around a single technical and semantic repository

standardization of experimentation, tracking, and validation using automated pipelines

integration with external systems for control, security, deployment, and monitoring

A common use case is found in financial institutions with multiple data squads operating in different domains: credit, risk, fraud prevention, marketing, customer relations, and investments. Each squad works with its own datasets, specific models, and distinct goals. MLflow, in this context, must be configured as a multi-user environment with logical isolation by project and integration with the corporate identity system. Using experiments organized by functional area, combined with author tags and consistent versioning structures, each squad can operate autonomously without losing institutional traceability.

Another standard found in digital retail companies is the use of MLflow as the backbone of personalization pipelines. Models for recommendation, segmentation, demand forecasting, and churn analysis are trained, validated, and deployed daily using CI/CD pipelines integrated with MLflow Projects. Metric tracking at scale is centralized, and artifacts are stored in buckets with hierarchy by date, model, and version. These environments use tools like Airflow or Prefect to schedule automated runs, invoke mlflow run with dynamic parameters, save artifacts, and programmatically decide whether the resulting version should be promoted to the Model Registry.

bash

```
mlflow run . -P data_path=s3://data/dataset_20250418.csv -P max_depth=8 -P lr=0.03
```

This command is executed nightly in batch by pipelines that fetch the previous day's data, train new models, and compare the obtained metrics with the previous Registry version. If the current model outperforms the production version, it is automatically promoted and deployed to the active endpoint.

Technology companies—especially platforms dealing with massive volumes of transactional or social data—use MLflow in hybrid environments with Spark, Delta Lake, and Kubernetes. The Tracking Server runs in dedicated pods with horizontal scalability and replicated databases. The backend store is a PostgreSQL database with multi-zone backups, and the artifact store is a bucket with automatic lifecycle policies to archive old files. Models are versioned with MLflow Models, containerized in Docker, and delivered via Istio in a microservices architecture.

These environments use standardized technical tags on each run:

- Model_author

- Dataset_version

- Pipeline_hash

- Execution_environment

- Model_type

- Training_time

- job_origin

This taxonomy allows data to be cross-referenced between runs, historical metrics to be traced, validation cycles to be audited, and analytical dashboards to be built based on real executions. MLflow's UI is complemented with visualizations in Grafana, Power BI, or Looker, connected via API to the metadata database.

Another approach in large corporations is to use MLflow for governance and compliance. In sectors like healthcare, telecommunications, and energy, legal requirements mandate traceability, explainability, and reproducibility. MLflow is used as a technical repository where every deployed model has a direct link to its code, dataset, parameters, environment, and author. All algorithmic decisions can be reconstructed. This is accomplished by storing:

- source code hash
- dataset version

- exact Conda environment configuration
- digital signature of the model version

This approach is integrated with audit and internal control systems. Executions are peer-reviewed before any promotion. Deployment scripts require formal approval, and inference logs are encrypted and indexed by user identifier.

In multinational operations, MLflow is configured with multiple Tracking Servers per region, synchronized by metadata replication and nightly merge pipelines. Each regional unit operates locally, but centrally approved models are promoted to a global Registry. This hybrid architecture ensures compliance with local legislation (e.g., data residency) without sacrificing global standardization.

A frequent challenge in these scenarios is **cost control**. In large-scale environments, hundreds of experiments are run weekly, generating gigabytes of artifacts. Version control, automatic cleanup of obsolete runs, file compression, and archiving policies are indispensable.

python

```python
from mlflow.tracking import MlflowClient


client = MlflowClient()
runs = client.search_runs("12345", filter_string="metrics.auc < 0.7 and tags.model_type='test'")
for run in runs:
    client.delete_run(run.info.run_id)
```

This script removes low-performance runs labeled as "test" and is scheduled weekly to keep storage usage in check.

Other observed large-scale use cases include:

- churn prediction with multiple models per customer cluster

- anomaly detection in IoT sensor networks with continuous data pipelines

- dynamic risk scoring in fintechs with daily model updates

- automated model selection by performance in A/B testing environments

- automatic version rotation based on meta-learning

These applications require MLflow to be fully integrated into the organization's technical stack. This includes integration with:

- CI/CD systems like GitLab, Jenkins, or Argo

- cloud providers like AWS, Azure, or GCP

- Kubernetes for container orchestration

- analytical databases like Snowflake, Redshift, or BigQuery

- authentication and authorization services like OAuth2, LDAP, or SSO

- observability tools like Datadog, Prometheus, or New Relic

Common Errors and Solutions

Error: "Tracking server overload"
Cause: Too many simultaneous connections in SQLite or misconfigured PostgreSQL
Recommended Solution: Migrate to a managed database with

pooling, apply replication and table partitioning

Error: "Loss of run context in concurrent jobs"
Cause: Parallel executions without isolated environment variables
Recommended Solution: Generate unique run_id per execution and pass it explicitly to scripts

Error: "Excess of unused artifacts"
Cause: No retention or compression policy
Recommended Solution: Implement cleanup scripts based on tags, age, and performance

Error: "Replication failure between regions"
Cause: Inconsistent file signatures or database replication latency
Recommended Solution: Automate nightly merge with hash integrity checks and semantic diffs

Error: "Registry version conflict"
Cause: Independent squads promoting models with the same name
Recommended Solution: Adopt a hierarchical naming convention like squad1/fraud_model and global/fraud_model

Best Practices

- Define naming standards for experiments, runs, models, and tags from the start

- Isolate environments by project or squad with distinct Tracking Server URIs

- Integrate MLflow with CI/CD pipelines with automatic validations, controlled deploys, and safe rollbacks

- Automate logging of critical metadata (dataset, author, environment, pipeline hash)

- Implement dashboards to track experimentation and model comparison

- Audit deployed models with versioned technical reports and source code links

- Document architecture, conventions, and cleanup routines as part of ML governance

- Ensure periodic backup of metadata and artifacts with restore testing

- Create a reusable repository of transformation, validation, and evaluation pipelines
- Maintain a dedicated team for the evolution of MLflow as an internal experimentation platform

Strategic Summary

Adopting MLflow in large-scale environments marks a leap in Machine Learning engineering maturity. It evolves from a tracking tool to an operational platform for experimentation, governance, and value delivery. With MLflow, models move beyond isolated scripts to become corporate assets—versioned, auditable, and reusable. The challenge is not only in scaling infrastructure, but in scaling processes, control, quality, and collective learning. The use cases described here show that, when well implemented, MLflow can support operations with dozens of teams, thousands of models, and billions of predictions—always with technical traceability, operational efficiency, and institutional security. Scaling is not just about running faster—it's about maintaining clarity, reliability, and control, even in the most complex environments.

CHAPTER 19. INTEGRATIONS WITH AUTOML

The advancement of AutoML platforms has significantly transformed the development cycle of Machine Learning models. By automating tasks such as algorithm selection, hyperparameter tuning, feature engineering, and cross-validation, these tools allow teams to deliver predictive solutions more quickly—especially in contexts of high demand, low technical maturity, or the need for rapid prototyping. However, adopting AutoML in structured environments requires integration with versioning, tracking, and governance tools. This is precisely where MLflow connects with strategic value: orchestrating and logging every experiment generated by AutoML platforms, ensuring traceability, control, and auditability—even when the model was not written manually.

Integrating AutoML with MLflow means turning a process that tends to be a "black box" into an auditable, transparent operation aligned with the engineering standards adopted by mature teams. The goal is not to replace data scientists but to enable automated solutions to integrate securely, traceably, and productively into the organization's Machine Learning pipeline.

The main AutoML frameworks with MLflow integration support are:

- H2O.ai AutoML

- Amazon SageMaker Autopilot

- Azure AutoML

- Google Cloud Vertex AI AutoML

- Databricks AutoML

- Auto-sklearn

- TPOT

- FLAML

- MLJAR

Each has technical particularities and varying levels of native integration, but all can be connected to MLflow via public APIs, custom wrappers, or manually registered artifacts.

In the case of H2O.ai, AutoML allows executing multiple models in parallel, applying cross-validation, filtering out ineffective algorithms, and returning the best models ranked by metric. Integration with MLflow can be done using mlflow.h2o.log_model() and manually logging parameters and metrics:

python

```
import mlflow
import mlflow.h2o


mlflow.set_experiment("automl_risco_credito")


with mlflow.start_run():
    aml = H2OAutoML(max_models=20, seed=1)
    aml.train(x=features, y=target, training_frame=train_data)
```

```
best_model = aml.leader

mlflow.h2o.log_model(best_model, "modelo_automl_h2o")

mlflow.log_metric("auc",
aml.leader.model_performance(test_data).auc())
```

This model is registered with all H2O artifacts and can be versioned, compared, promoted in the Registry, and exposed as an API.

In Azure, azureml-automl has direct integration with MLflow via the SDK. Once an AutoML task execution is complete, the best model can be automatically published to the Azure ML workspace and simultaneously registered in MLflow:

python

```python
from azureml.train.automl import AutoMLConfig

from azureml.core import Experiment

from azureml.core.workspace import Workspace


automl_config = AutoMLConfig(
    task='classification',
    primary_metric='AUC_weighted',
    experiment_timeout_minutes=30,
    training_data=dataset,
    label_column_name='target',
    n_cross_validations=5)
```

```
exp = Experiment(ws, 'automl_experimento_credito')
run = exp.submit(automl_config, show_output=True)
best_run, fitted_model = run.get_output()


import mlflow.azureml
mlflow.azureml.log_model(fitted_model,
"modelo_automl_azure")
```

Google Cloud's AutoML, via Vertex AI, allows exporting trained models in SavedModel or XGBoost format, which can be logged in MLflow via mlflow.tensorflow.log_model() or mlflow.xgboost.log_model():

python

```
import mlflow.xgboost


mlflow.set_experiment("credito_vertex_ai")


with mlflow.start_run():
    model = xgboost.Booster()
    model.load_model("model.bst")
    mlflow.xgboost.log_model(model,
"modelo_vertex_exportado")
```

This practice ensures that even externally trained models can be brought into the MLflow tracking structure, associated with tags, metrics, and additional parameters.

For frameworks like Auto-sklearn or TPOT, which operate locally and generate optimized pipelines, the integration process involves encapsulating the final model, saving the parameters used, and logging the results:

python

```python
import mlflow.sklearn
from autosklearn.classification import AutoSklearnClassifier

mlflow.set_experiment("automl_sklearn_credito")

with mlflow.start_run():
    model = AutoSklearnClassifier(time_left_for_this_task=360)
    model.fit(X_train, y_train)

    mlflow.sklearn.log_model(model, "modelo_autosklearn")
    mlflow.log_metric("f1", f1_score(y_test, model.predict(X_test)))
```

The same applies to TPOT, where the generated pipeline is converted into a sklearn estimator and logged with mlflow.sklearn.log_model().

An important point when integrating AutoML with MLflow is logging all attempted runs, not just the best model. This can be done using nested runs or separate artifacts containing the full ranking of executions, execution times, and tested hyperparameters. This way, the final selection is traceable and auditable:

python

```
with mlflow.start_run() as parent_run:
    for i, modelo in enumerate(lista_modelos_testados):
        with mlflow.start_run(nested=True):
            mlflow.log_metric("f1", modelo.f1_score)
            mlflow.log_param("algoritmo", modelo.algoritmo)
            mlflow.log_param("tempo_execucao", modelo.tempo)
```

Additionally, comparing AutoML models with manually built models must be done fairly. AutoML often produces high-performance models with extremely complex pipelines, which may be hard to interpret and slower in inference. MLflow helps document these characteristics and supports business decisions based on objective trade-offs.

Another critical point is deployment. Since not all AutoML-generated models are compatible with MLflow's native flavors, it may be necessary to create a custom wrapper for mlflow.pyfunc, defining how the model is loaded and how it performs predictions:

python

```
import mlflow.pyfunc


class ModeloAutoMLWrapper(mlflow.pyfunc.PythonModel):
    def load_context(self, context):
        import joblib
        self.model = joblib.load(context.artifacts["modelo_arquivo"])
```

```
def predict(self, context, model_input):
    return self.model.predict(model_input)


mlflow.pyfunc.log_model(
    artifact_path="modelo_wrapped",
    python_model=ModeloAutoMLWrapper(),
    artifacts={"modelo_arquivo": "path/model.joblib"}
)
```

This wrapper ensures compatibility with standard MLflow Models prediction endpoints, allowing deployment with mlflow models serve or export to Docker containers.

Common Errors and Solutions

Error: "NotImplementedError: No flavor backend found for model type"
Probable cause: Attempting to log an AutoML model in an unsupported format
Recommended solution: Create a custom wrapper with mlflow.pyfunc.PythonModel

Error: "MemoryError during AutoML run"
Probable cause: Execution on a machine with insufficient resources
Recommended solution: Limit the number of models or use a cloud environment with autoscaling

Error: "Model missing required methods predict or transform"
Probable cause: Model not following sklearn standard or not serialized properly

Recommended solution: Validate model signature and adapt pipeline with expected methods

Error: "Model too large for Registry upload"
Probable cause: Model has too many sub-artifacts, checkpoints, or embedded components
Recommended solution: Compress, clean redundant artifacts, or export only essential parts

Error: "Metric comparison failed due to missing values"
Probable cause: AutoML returned incomplete pipelines in some runs
Recommended solution: Filter only valid runs before logging or comparing models

Best Practices

- Log all tested models—not just the best—along with metrics and hyperparameters

- Export AutoML execution logs as MLflow artifacts for traceability

- Document AutoML model limitations, including inference time, interpretability, and pipeline complexity

- Integrate AutoML with CI/CD pipelines for continuous evaluation and automatic promotion based on metrics

- Use specific tags to distinguish AutoML executions from manual ones

- Evaluate performance versus interpretability, especially in regulated contexts

- Avoid AutoML pipeline overfitting with internal validation—always validate on separate datasets

- Encapsulate AutoML pipelines with preprocessing identical to the production environment

- Version the AutoML execution script explicitly to ensure replicability

- Validate MLflow Models compatibility before deployment to avoid operational surprises

Strategic Summary

Integrating AutoML with MLflow combines the speed and convenience of automation with the robustness and traceability of applied engineering. AutoML accelerates the discovery of competitive models, but MLflow ensures those models are auditable, versioned, governed, and production-ready. In corporate environments, this combination is decisive for democratizing modeling without compromising quality. By documenting each step, logging every metric, and standardizing deployment, this integration transforms automated solutions into reliable assets aligned with the technical strategy and the continuous improvement cycle. *AutoML without traceability is agility with risk. AutoML with MLflow is speed with accountability.*

CHAPTER 20. EXPERIMENT REPRODUCIBILITY AND AUDITABILITY

Machine Learning projects that cannot be reproduced are technically broken. The ability to repeat an execution and obtain the same results is the foundation upon which trust in any algorithmic solution is built. Reproducibility is not just a technical requirement, but a strategic necessity in regulated environments, distributed teams, and mission-critical contexts. Auditing, in turn, is the extension of this logic: it is the ability to investigate, justify, and validate every decision made by a model. MLflow offers a solid foundation to ensure reproducibility and auditing through comprehensive run tracking, artifact versioning, environment encapsulation, and source code integration.

Reproducibility in Machine Learning requires three fundamental conditions:

- preserved and versioned input data

- registered and fixed transformation code and logic

- controlled execution environment (dependencies, operating system, parameters)

If any of these three dimensions vary, re-execution may yield a different result. MLflow's core function is to log these three layers as part of each run, creating a complete technical trace that allows reproducing the execution in any other environment with the same context.

In MLflow, each run is identified by a unique run_id, linked to:

- parameters (log_param)

- metrics (log_metric)

- artifacts (log_artifact)

- trained model (log_model)

- source code (log_artifact or set_tag)

- environment (conda.yaml or Dockerfile)

- execution date and time

- additional metadata tags

With these records, it is possible to reconstruct the full state of an execution, even years later.

Environment encapsulation is done using mlflow.projects, which defines in the MLproject file the project structure, dependencies, and execution command. The use of conda_env or docker_env ensures that re-execution is performed in an identical environment:

yaml

```yaml
name: projeto_credito
conda_env: conda.yaml
entry_points:
  main:
    parameters:
```

```
    max_depth: {type: int, default: 5}
  command: >
    python treino.py --max_depth {max_depth}
```

This manifest can be executed with mlflow run, locally, on a remote machine, or through a pipeline:

bash

```
mlflow run . -P max_depth=7
```

Reproducibility is guaranteed as long as the source code and input data remain intact. To achieve this, it is essential to version these files and register their hashes as tags in MLflow:

python

```
import hashlib


def hash_arquivo(caminho):
    with open(caminho, "rb") as f:
        return hashlib.sha256(f.read()).hexdigest()


mlflow.set_tag("hash_treino", hash_arquivo("treino.py"))
mlflow.set_tag("hash_dataset", hash_arquivo("dados.csv"))
```

This hash allows later validation of whether the files used in a new run are the same as in the original execution.

Another strategy is to save the actual files as artifacts:

python

```python
mlflow.log_artifact("treino.py")
mlflow.log_artifact("dados.csv")
```

This way, the files used are stored with the run and can be inspected, downloaded, or reused in new tests.

For auditing, logging the author and purpose of the execution is essential. This can be done using custom tags:

python

```python
mlflow.set_tag("executado_por", "carlos.ferreira")
mlflow.set_tag("finalidade", "validação_prod")
mlflow.set_tag("versao_pipeline", "v3.1.2")
```

These tags allow generating filtered reports, identifying decisions made by individuals or teams, and tracking the evolution of experiments over time.

Auditing also extends to stage transition logging in the Model Registry. Each promotion of a model to Staging or Production should be recorded with a clear description:

python

```python
client.transition_model_version_stage(
    name="ClassificadorCredito",
    version=3,
    stage="Production",
    archive_existing_versions=True
)


client.update_model_version(
```

```
    name="ClassificadorCredito",

    version=3,

    description="Promovido após aprovação do comitê de risco
em 2025-03-22"

)
```

This comment is recorded as part of the model's history, allowing the reconstruction of the technical rationale behind each deploy.

In regulated contexts such as banking, healthcare, or energy, auditing requires that every deployed model be associated with:

- versioned and auditable dataset

- documented and immutable source code

- recorded statistical validation

- formal technical approval process

- access control and execution logs

- rollback plan in case of regression

MLflow facilitates implementing these requirements by centralizing technical metadata and offering flexible integration with external systems.

A good practice in auditable environments is to generate an automated technical document per execution, with a run summary, used parameters, main metrics, referenced dataset, applied code, generated model, and direct link to the run in MLflow.

This report can be generated in HTML or PDF and saved as an artifact:

python

```python
with open("relatorio_execucao.html", "w") as f:
    f.write(conteudo_html)


mlflow.log_artifact("relatorio_execucao.html")
```

This type of technical evidence is valuable for internal audits, certifications, quality processes, and incident investigations.

Another important point is comparing runs. MLflow allows comparing metrics across multiple runs, either visually or via code. This enables identifying regressions, improvements, or the impact of specific changes:

python

```python
from mlflow.tracking import MlflowClient


client = MlflowClient()
runs = client.search_runs(
    experiment_ids=["0"],
    filter_string="tags.finalidade = 'validação_prod'",
    order_by=["metrics.f1 DESC"]
)
```

These queries allow extracting technical insights, justifying versioning decisions, and structuring technical presentations based on real and auditable data.

Reproducibility also requires data used to be accessible. This can be achieved by versioning datasets in systems like DVC, LakeFS, or Delta Lake, and logging the corresponding hash or commit as a tag in MLflow:

python

```
mlflow.set_tag("dvc_commit", "a84f7e3b87a1db1a36e...")
```

Thus, even if the data is not stored as an artifact, it is possible to trace exactly which data was used, as long as it is stored in an external versioned repository.

Common Errors and Solutions

Error: "Results differ from previous run with same parameters"
Probable cause: Different execution environment, altered library version, or modified data
Recommended solution: Log conda.yaml, save dataset as artifact, or log hash

Error: "Run not reproducible due to missing artifact"
Probable cause: Deleted artifact or moved artifact bucket
Recommended solution: Ensure regular backup and versioning of critical artifacts

Error: "Metrics inconsistent after retrain"
Probable cause: Random seed not fixed
Recommended solution: Set random_state or global seed in all executions

Error: "Unclear origin of model in production"
Probable cause: Model promoted without linking to a registered run
Recommended solution: Link model to run ID and add description with technical justification

Error: "Dataset path changed, breaking retrain process"

Probable cause: Non-versioned data path or dependency on local environment

Recommended solution: Use stable URIs or version data in DVC or LakeFS

Best Practices

- Log conda.yaml, requirements.txt, or Dockerfile as part of each run

- Save the source code used as an artifact or log its hash as a tag

- Version data using external tools and link the commit or URI in MLflow

- Create automated technical reports and save them as run artifacts

- Document all parameters, including non-optimized ones, to ensure accurate repetition

- Enforce use of fixed random seeds to ensure determinism

- Mark auditable runs with a specific tag for easier search and tracking

- Avoid running models via loose scripts; always use mlflow run with a manifest

- Validate the environment with automatic checks of library versions at execution start

- Periodically simulate re-execution of past runs to validate true reproducibility

Strategic Summary

Reproducibility and experiment auditing are not technical details—they are the foundations of trustworthy Machine Learning engineering. Ensuring that an execution can be repeated, explained, validated, and audited turns models from scripts into operational assets. MLflow provides the structure for this, but it is technical rigor and a documentation culture that make this structure effective. In environments where algorithmic decisions impact finance, healthcare, justice, or critical infrastructure, there is no room for opaque models or unverifiable results. To reproduce is to prove. To audit is to protect. And logging every step is what separates amateur experimentation from professional operation.

CHAPTER 21. CREATING EXTENSIONS AND PLUGINS

Although MLflow is robust and complete in its core structure, it is designed to be extensible. This characteristic makes it adaptable to different domains, architectures, and operational requirements. Creating extensions and plugins is the key to tailoring MLflow to the specific realities of each organization, team, or project. With extensions, it is possible to connect new model formats, integrate with proprietary tools, build custom automation layers, implement additional security controls, or add specific validations to the pipeline logic. This chapter presents, in a technical and applied manner, how to safely and modularly extend MLflow in alignment with the TECHWRITE 2.2 Protocol.

MLflow's architecture supports extension primarily in three layers:

- **Flavors**: definition of new model types with their log, load, and predict methods.

- **CLI Plugins**: custom commands that integrate into the mlflow terminal.

- **Custom Python Models (mlflow.pyfunc)**: encapsulation of custom logic for prediction, transformation, or control.

Creating a new flavor allows any framework, library, or model format to be integrated with MLflow. This is useful when wanting to version, register, and serve models built with tools outside the standard ecosystem, such as LightGBM, Prophet, CatBoost, H2O, PyCaret, or proprietary internal models.

The basic structure of a flavor includes:

- log method (log_model)

- load method (load_model)

- definition of how to save the artifact

- specification in the MLmodel file

A flavor is technically a Python module with standardized functions and an expected directory structure.

python

```python
def    log_model(model,    artifact_path,    conda_env=None,
**kwargs):
    # save the model to disk
    path = os.path.join(artifact_path, "model.mymodel")
    with open(path, "wb") as f:
        f.write(model.serialize())
    mlflow.log_artifact(path, artifact_path)

    # generate MLmodel file with the specification
    mlflow_model = Model()
    mlflow_model.add_flavor("my_custom_flavor",
model_file="model.mymodel")
    mlflow_model.save(os.path.join(artifact_path, "MLmodel"))
```

The MLmodel file defines the flavor and how the model will be loaded, ensuring compatibility with the mlflow models serve interface.

Creating a CLI plugin allows specific commands to be added to the MLflow command line. It is possible to create commands like mlflow lint-model, mlflow validate-data, or mlflow export-stats, which encapsulate internal organizational logic.

To do this, you must create a Python package with the entry point configured in setup.py:

python

```
entry_points={

    "mlflow.project_backend": [

        "validate = my_plugins.validate:cli"

    ]

}
```

The cli() command is then registered and invoked directly via the MLflow terminal.

The third and most common form of extension is creating custom models using mlflow.pyfunc.PythonModel. This allows any prediction logic to be encapsulated within MLflow's standardized interface, ensuring compatibility with the Registry, REST deploy, Docker export, and production serving.

python

```
import mlflow.pyfunc


class MeuModeloWrapper(mlflow.pyfunc.PythonModel):
```

```python
    def load_context(self, context):
        import joblib
        self.modelo =
joblib.load(context.artifacts["modelo_serializado"])


    def predict(self, context, model_input):
        preprocessado = self.preprocessamento(model_input)
        return self.modelo.predict(preprocessado)


    def preprocessamento(self, dados):
        # transformation logic
        return dados
```

This model can be logged with:

python

```python
mlflow.pyfunc.log_model(
    artifact_path="modelo_pipeline",
    python_model=MeuModeloWrapper(),
    artifacts={"modelo_serializado": "modelo.pkl"}
)
```

This pattern is used to apply transformations before prediction, inject validation logic, compose multiple models in sequence, or integrate with external sources at inference time.

When creating extensions, it is important to document expected behavior, accepted parameters, required environment, and side effects. Every extension should have:

- automated tests covering valid and invalid inputs

- structured logging with configurable detail level

- fail-safes for edge cases

- dependency isolation

In corporate environments, it is recommended to centralize plugins in an internal repository, with versioning and an approval process. This avoids unorganized extension growth and ensures technical quality.

Another strategic use of extensions is to create custom validators. Functions can be built to analyze the model, dataset, or environment before promotion to the Registry. This can be integrated as a hook in CI/CD pipelines.

python

```python
def validar_modelo(model_path):
    modelo = joblib.load(model_path)
    if hasattr(modelo, "coef_") and modelo.coef_.sum() == 0:
        raise ValueError("Null model cannot be promoted")
```

This function can be called before each log_model, preventing technically or logically flawed models from being registered.

It is also possible to create components that validate the execution environment, detecting incompatible library versions or incorrect hardware configurations.

In deployment pipelines, it is common to integrate plugins that:

- check compatibility between model input and expected payload

- validate minimum performance using simulated production data

- calculate ethical metrics, such as group bias or fairness score

- generate automated technical documentation as an artifact

These practices increase process reliability and reduce rework caused by insecure or poorly documented deployments.

Common Errors and Solutions

Error: "ModuleNotFoundError in custom PythonModel"
Probable cause: Dependency not declared in conda.yaml
Recommended solution: Explicitly add all libraries to the environment

Error: "predict() returned NoneType"
Probable cause: Internal logic with no return in all possible branches
Recommended solution: Validate return coverage in all function paths

Error: "Plugin not registered in entry_points"
Probable cause: Failure in Python package setup
Recommended solution: Review setup.py and ensure correct mapping in entry_points

Error: "Flavor not recognized" when serving custom model
Probable cause: Missing correct specification in the MLmodel file
Recommended solution: Generate the MLmodel with all desired

flavors and point to correct files

Error: "Conda environment not found" when executing custom model
Probable cause: Execution without defining conda_env when logging the model
Recommended solution: Create and log the environment with mlflow.pyfunc.log_model(..., conda_env="env.yaml")

Best Practices

- Create reusable wrappers for preprocessing, validation, and input transformation

- Document all extensions with usage examples, signature, and functional scope

- Use detailed logs with logging and separation by level (INFO, WARNING, ERROR)

- Isolate plugin dependencies in specific Conda environments to avoid conflicts

- Test extensions with real data and failure simulations before production use

- Version each plugin as a Python package with release control and changelog

- Create an internal catalog of extensions with functional description, owner, and maintenance status

- Avoid hardcoded values in plugins; parameterize behavior whenever possible

- Integrate custom validators into CI/CD steps with

automatic blocking of invalid versions

- Monitor plugin usage via optional telemetry (opt-in) to detect obsolescence or low adoption

Strategic Summary

Creating extensions and plugins in MLflow is the bridge between the generic platform and the operational reality of each organization. By extending MLflow, technical teams can adapt the model lifecycle to their own business, compliance, architecture, and domain requirements. This transforms MLflow into a living platform that grows with the team's maturity and the complexity of its challenges. Well-built plugins increase productivity, reduce errors, enforce standards, and create reusable operational intelligence. Extensibility is not about adding complexity—it's about scaling control, adaptability, and value. And when done with technical rigor, each extension becomes an accelerator of trust and consistency in the model lifecycle.

CHAPTER 22. INTEGRATION WITH SPARK AND BIG DATA

Machine Learning projects that operate on large volumes of data require architectures compatible with distributed processing, task parallelization, and horizontal scalability. Apache Spark is the primary processing engine for these demands, offering native support for data pipelines, large-scale transformations, and distributed execution of machine learning algorithms. Integrating MLflow with Spark and Big Data environments allows for experiment tracking, model versioning, and solution operationalization without compromising performance or governance. This chapter technically details how to structure the integration between MLflow, Spark, and large-scale data volumes in compliance with the TECHWRITE 2.2 Protocol.

MLflow integration with Spark can be implemented at different levels:

- tracking experiments that use Spark MLlib or custom algorithms with RDDs and DataFrames

- logging and versioning models generated with MLlib (mlflow.spark.log_model)

- executing projects with mlflow run over Spark clusters via spark-submit

- encapsulating distributed preprocessing and transformation with PySpark in pyfunc models

- logging distributed metrics in scalable data pipelines

When using Spark as the training engine, it's essential to ensure the execution context is connected to the MLflow Tracking Server so that each run is properly logged even in managed clusters such as Databricks, EMR, GCP Dataproc, or Azure Synapse.

python

```python
from pyspark.sql import SparkSession
import mlflow
import mlflow.spark


spark = SparkSession.builder.appName("modelo_risco_credito").getOrCreate()
mlflow.set_tracking_uri("http://mlflow.seu-dominio.com")
mlflow.set_experiment("credito_bigdata")


with mlflow.start_run():
    df = spark.read.parquet("s3://dados/credito_historico")


    from pyspark.ml.feature import VectorAssembler
    from pyspark.ml.classification import RandomForestClassifier


    assembler = VectorAssembler(inputCols=["idade", "renda", "score"], outputCol="features")
    dados = assembler.transform(df)
```

```
modelo = RandomForestClassifier(labelCol="inadimplente",
featuresCol="features")

modelo_treinado = modelo.fit(dados)


mlflow.spark.log_model(modelo_treinado,
"modelo_rf_spark")

mlflow.log_param("numTrees", modelo.getNumTrees())

mlflow.log_param("maxDepth", modelo.getMaxDepth())
```

This code logs not only the model but also the parameters and the trained artifact, which will be serialized in MLlib format and can later be reloaded with mlflow.spark.load_model.

The saved model can be reused for batch scoring on distributed data:

python

```
modelo_carregado        =        mlflow.spark.load_model("runs:/
<run_id>/modelo_rf_spark")

resultado = modelo_carregado.transform(novos_dados)
```

The result can be saved directly to distributed file systems:

python

```
resultado.write.mode("overwrite").parquet("s3://saida/
predicoes_20250420")
```

The execution of Spark pipelines can be tracked via MLflow Projects, using spark-submit in the entry_point of the manifest:

yaml

```
name: modelo_spark_pipeline

entry_points:
  main:
    parameters:
      input_path: {type: str}
      output_path: {type: str}
    command: >
      spark-submit pipeline.py --input {input_path} --output {output_path}
```

This project can be executed with:

bash

```
mlflow run . -P input_path=s3://dados/entrada -P output_path=s3://resultados/predicoes
```

This pattern allows complex pipelines to be re-executed with automatic tracking, parameter control, and code versioning.

Another important strategy is encapsulating Spark transformations inside pyfunc models so that preprocessing can be reused in deployment. This is useful when part of the model logic depends on distributed pipelines or specific normalizations.

python

```
import mlflow.pyfunc

from pyspark.sql import DataFrame
```

```python
class ModeloSparkWrapper(mlflow.pyfunc.PythonModel):
    def load_context(self, context):
        self.spark = SparkSession.builder.getOrCreate()
        self.modelo =
mlflow.spark.load_model(context.artifacts["modelo_spark"])


    def predict(self, context, model_input):
        df_spark = self.spark.createDataFrame(model_input)
        return self.modelo.transform(df_spark).toPandas()
["prediction"]


mlflow.pyfunc.log_model(
    artifact_path="modelo_wrapper",
    python_model=ModeloSparkWrapper(),
    artifacts={"modelo_spark": "runs:/<run_id>/
modelo_rf_spark"}
)
```

This model can be served via mlflow models serve, receiving Pandas format inputs and applying Spark transformations in the backend.

Distributed pipeline monitoring can also be integrated into MLflow through custom metric logs:

python

```python
mlflow.log_metric("linhas_processadas", df.count())
```

```
mlflow.log_metric("tempo_treino",
tempo_execucao.total_seconds())
```

These metrics can be collected and compared across runs, enabling performance, efficiency, and cost analysis per batch.

In environments such as Databricks, MLflow is already natively integrated with Spark, allowing any notebook or distributed job to automatically log its experiments without additional configuration.

Common Errors and Solutions

Error: "No tracking URI set" when using Spark standalone
Probable cause: Spark environment not configured with MLflow URI
Recommended solution: Define mlflow.set_tracking_uri at the beginning of the Spark session

Error: "Model not serializable" when trying to log pipeline
Probable cause: Spark pipeline contains unsupported custom transformations
Recommended solution: Ensure all pipeline stages are serializable and MLlib-compatible

Error: "SparkSession not found" when serving model
Probable cause: pyfunc model expects Spark context but is being executed in a local environment
Recommended solution: Configure the deployment environment with Spark or encapsulate logic in Pandas

Error: "Out of memory" when applying transformations on large volumes
Probable cause: Unnecessary conversion from Spark DataFrame to Pandas
Recommended solution: Keep processing in Spark whenever

possible and avoid .toPandas()

Error: "Missing JAR" when executing spark-submit with MLlib
Probable cause: Environment missing standard MLlib libraries
Recommended solution: Use container or cluster with full Spark
image including MLlib dependencies

Best Practices

- Version all scripts used in the Spark pipeline and log them as artifacts

- Ensure each Spark execution is tracked with a unique ID and associated with the corresponding project

- Use MLlib's VectorAssembler and Pipeline to encapsulate transformations with compatibility

- Store execution metrics, processing time, and data volume as part of the run context

- Integrate Spark jobs with MLflow via Airflow, Prefect, or Databricks Jobs for scheduled and controlled repetition

- Avoid dependency on local environment—always validate script portability to managed clusters

- Reuse Spark models logged with mlflow.spark.log_model for batch scoring and pyfunc APIs

- Document parameters used and data origin with technical tags and referential artifacts

- Automate performance testing with sampled datasets to prevent scale regressions

- Configure alerts for execution failures, long runtimes, or unexpected data volume shifts

Strategic Summary

Integrating MLflow with Spark and Big Data environments is essential for projects that deal with volume, variety, and velocity. This integration allows experiments to be tracked even in distributed pipelines, models to be versioned even with parallel logic, and large-scale predictions to be audited and optimized. MLflow makes the model lifecycle in Spark as traceable as in local environments—without losing processing elasticity. When well implemented, this integration turns a distributed cluster into a continuous experimentation platform, where every processed row generates learning, control, and value.

CHAPTER 23. HYPERPARAMETER OPTIMIZATION

Choosing the right hyperparameters can determine the success or failure of a Machine Learning model. Even with good data and an appropriate algorithm, ineffective hyperparameter configurations can lead to underperforming models, poor generalization, or excessive training time. Hyperparameter optimization is the systematic process of testing different parameter combinations to maximize a target metric, ensuring the best possible performance of a model on a given dataset. MLflow offers robust support to manage, track, and compare these runs, making the process efficient, reproducible, and auditable.

Hyperparameters differ from internal model parameters. They are not learned during training but are set beforehand. Common examples include:

- maximum depth of trees in tree-based models

- learning rate in optimization algorithms

- number of estimators in ensembles

- loss function or penalty

- splitting criteria in decision trees

- number of neurons or layers in neural networks

The most naive optimization strategy is grid search, where all possible combinations of a fixed set of values are tested. While simple, this approach is computationally expensive and does not scale well with multiple hyperparameters. More efficient alternatives include:

- random search: random combinations within a defined space

- Bayesian optimization: probabilistic functions to estimate the best region

- evolutionary algorithms: iterative mutations and selections based on performance

- early stopping: halting runs with low partial performance

- learning-based methods, such as Hyperband and BOHB

MLflow's integration with optimization tools allows automatic logging of each run with its respective hyperparameters, metrics, and artifacts, facilitating post-analysis and selection of the best combination.

A basic integration pattern involves executing multiple MLflow runs, each with a different hyperparameter set:

python

```
import mlflow
from sklearn.ensemble import RandomForestClassifier
from sklearn.metrics import f1_score

parametros = [
    {"max_depth": 4, "n_estimators": 100},
```

```
    {"max_depth": 6, "n_estimators": 200},
    {"max_depth": 8, "n_estimators": 150}
]


for param in parametros:
    with mlflow.start_run():
        modelo = RandomForestClassifier(
            max_depth=param["max_depth"],
            n_estimators=param["n_estimators"]
        )
        modelo.fit(X_train, y_train)
        pred = modelo.predict(X_test)
        score = f1_score(y_test, pred)

        mlflow.log_params(param)
        mlflow.log_metric("f1_score", score)
        mlflow.sklearn.log_model(modelo, "modelo_rf")
```

Each execution is recorded with the tested values and resulting metric, enabling ordering and comparative analysis.

For more complex scenarios, it's common to use libraries such as:

- scikit-learn with GridSearchCV or RandomizedSearchCV

- Optuna with Bayesian search and automatic pruning

- Hyperopt with defined search spaces and parallel trials

- Ray Tune for distributed experiment execution

- Ax from Meta (Facebook) for adaptive optimization

MLflow can be integrated with these libraries via callbacks or custom wrappers. For example, Optuna has native integration with MLflow:

python

```python
import optuna
import mlflow

def objetivo(trial):
    n_estimators = trial.suggest_int("n_estimators", 50, 300)
    max_depth = trial.suggest_int("max_depth", 4, 12)

    modelo = RandomForestClassifier(n_estimators=n_estimators, max_depth=max_depth)
    modelo.fit(X_train, y_train)
    score = f1_score(y_test, modelo.predict(X_test))

    mlflow.log_param("n_estimators", n_estimators)
    mlflow.log_param("max_depth", max_depth)
    mlflow.log_metric("f1_score", score)

    return score
```

```
optuna.integration.mlflow.track_integration()
study = optuna.create_study(direction="maximize")
study.optimize(objetivo, n_trials=30)
```

This process creates an MLflow run for each Optuna trial with complete tracking.

Using mlflow.log_params() and mlflow.log_metric() ensures that all executions are organized and comparable within the MLflow interface, allowing filtering, metric-based sorting, and visual navigation of experiment evolution.

Additionally, each run can save intermediate artifacts—such as confusion matrices, ROC curves, or validation logs—supporting auditability and diagnostics.

Another useful pattern is to group experiments by parent run using nested=True, allowing all optimization runs to be grouped under a single parent:

python

```
with mlflow.start_run() as parent:
    for param in combinacoes:
        with mlflow.start_run(nested=True):
            # training and logging logic
```

This practice simplifies later analysis by linking all executions from a single optimization campaign.

Choosing the right target metric is also critical. Metrics like accuracy can be misleading in some projects. It's advisable to use metrics that reflect the model's real impact on the business, such as:

- F1 for imbalanced problems

- ROC AUC for discrimination assessment

- LogLoss for calibration

- estimated cost per error when errors have weighted impact

Cross-validation during optimization is another key aspect to avoid overfitting to test data and ensure good generalization:

python

```python
from sklearn.model_selection import cross_val_score


score = cross_val_score(modelo, X, y, cv=5, scoring="f1").mean()
mlflow.log_metric("f1_cv", score)
```

With multiple experiments recorded, you can use MlflowClient to retrieve the best model:

python

```python
from mlflow.tracking import MlflowClient


client = MlflowClient()
runs = client.search_runs(experiment_ids=["1"],
order_by=["metrics.f1_score DESC"])
melhor_run = runs[0]
print(melhor_run.data.params, melhor_run.data.metrics)
```

This model can then be directly loaded for inference or promoted to production via the Registry.

Common Errors and Solutions

Error: "ResourceExhaustedError" during optimization
Probable Cause: too many simultaneous runs.
Recommended solution: limit parallel n_trials or use distributed execution via Ray or Dask.

Error: "No best model found"
Probable Cause: all runs failed or errored during fit().
Recommended solution: verify search space and add exception handling during trials.

Error: *"Tracking URI not set"*
Probable Cause: environment without mlflow.set_tracking_uri().
Recommended solution: define the URI before launching trials.

Error: "Duplicate param key"
Probable Cause: same parameter logged multiple times.
Recommended solution: consolidate parameters before calling log_params.

Error: "Run not found when promoting best model"
Probable Cause: run_id not saved correctly or run deleted.
Recommended solution: save the winning run_id and protect it from auto-deletion.

Best Practices

- Use cross-validation as the metric during optimization for greater robustness.

- Log all relevant hyperparameters, even fixed ones, to simplify future comparisons.

- Group optimizations by project, task, or dataset version with clear tags and names.

- Avoid hardcoded values in training scripts—use external parameter configuration.

- Include training time and memory usage as part of evaluation.

- Use nested runs to maintain hierarchical organization of experiments.

- Visually analyze results with exported logs and interactive graphs.

- Monitor optimization convergence and stop campaigns with marginal gains.

- Implement automatic retry for trials that fail due to transient errors.

- Store execution logs and auxiliary files as artifacts for future diagnostics.

Strategic Summary

Hyperparameter optimization is a fundamental pillar of building robust, scalable, and competitive models. MLflow turns this process from chaotic, empirical, and opaque into something structured, traceable, and auditable. Each recorded run becomes a unit of technical learning. Every logged metric becomes a decision point. When well-integrated, optimization becomes a continuous engine of model evolution—where every attempt is documented and every improvement validated. In mature teams, hyperparameter selection is not art—it's data-driven engineering, backed by reliable, versioned, and reproducible processes. MLflow transforms trial and error into a systematic cycle of algorithmic improvement.

CHAPTER 24. RISK ANALYSIS AND CONTINGENCY PLANS

Machine Learning models, once deployed in production, operate under unpredictable conditions. Changes in data behavior, infrastructure failures, prediction errors, integration instabilities, and even malicious manipulation can compromise performance, trust, and operational continuity. In critical environments such as finance, healthcare, security, or infrastructure, these risks are not mere possibilities—they are real threats that must be identified, quantified, and mitigated in advance. Risk analysis and contingency planning are indispensable components of any robust MLOps strategy. MLflow, by structuring the model lifecycle with traceability and versioning, is a central tool to support these prevention, response, and recovery processes.

Risk analysis in Machine Learning projects can be organized into four major categories:

technical risks — code failures, drift, overfitting, pipeline bugs, loss of reproducibility

operational risks — endpoint unavailability, response latency, auxiliary service outages

data risks — leakage of sensitive information, inconsistent inputs, distribution shifts, lack of updates

business risks — negative impact on KPIs, incorrect decisions, reputational damage, discriminatory effects

Each of these categories requires different detection, response, and mitigation mechanisms. A technical contingency plan must include everything from automatic model rollback to backup activation and forced revalidation.

The first step in structuring contingency plans is identifying the pipeline's critical points. Which components, if failed, compromise the final result? Which depend on external services? Where is there a risk of receiving invalid or outdated input data?

From this mapping, a risk matrix is defined with three variables:

- likelihood of occurrence
- estimated impact on the system
- estimated time to recovery (TTR)

A high-probability, high-impact risk demands an immediate contingency plan. A low-impact, high-frequency risk may justify containment automation.

MLflow supports this structure by ensuring:

- tracking of all executions with technical context
- model versioning with simple rollback by stage
- metric and parameter logging to detect degradation
- complete auditability in case of incidents

Technically, the first risk to control is undetected drift. A model may be in production, responding normally, while its performance is gradually deteriorating due to changes in input data. Detecting data drift and concept drift must be part of continuous monitoring. If detected, the contingency plan may include:

- freezing the current deployment
- notifying the technical team
- promoting a previously validated alternative model
- forcing revalidation with a real production sample

Another common risk is prediction pipeline failure, which may occur due to:

- timeout from auxiliary services
- API version mismatch
- errors loading the model or dependencies
- corruption of the model or artifacts

In these cases, the contingency plan must be automatic and may involve:

- fallback to a previous model (last stable version)
- returning a parametrized default response
- logging the incident and pausing the inference flow
- escalation for manual review

MLflow supports fallback via model versioning in the Model Registry. A script can be triggered automatically to demote the current model and restore the last Production model that passed critical tests.

python

```
from mlflow.tracking import MlflowClient


client = MlflowClient()
versions = client.search_model_versions("name='modelo_fraude'")
prod_versions = [v for v in versions if v.current_stage == "Production"]
if not passed_test(current_v):
    client.transition_model_version_stage("modelo_fraude",
```

```python
version=current_v, stage="Archived")
    client.transition_model_version_stage("modelo_fraude",
version=prod_versions[-1], stage="Production")
```

This script can be triggered by a webhook, scheduler, or event detected in monitoring.

Another critical risk is the lack of reproducibility during incident analysis. When a serious error occurs, the team must be able to re-execute the model with the same data, code, and parameters as the original run. This is only possible if MLflow is correctly configured with artifact, code, and environment logging.

python

```python
mlflow.log_artifact("dataset_sample.csv")

mlflow.log_artifact("inference_code.py")

mlflow.set_tag("pipeline_version", "v3.2.1")
```

If the incident is caused by performance regression, it's possible to quickly compare past runs using the MLflow client:

python

```python
runs = client.search_runs(experiment_ids=["5"],
order_by=["metrics.auc DESC"])

for run in runs:
    print(run.info.run_id, run.data.metrics["auc"])
```

If an older model shows better performance, it can be restored with a single command, reducing downtime.

Besides performance, ethical and regulatory risks must also be considered. A model that starts to systematically discriminate against certain groups may have legal consequences. It is crucial to apply fairness tests and segmented impact analysis regularly. The contingency plan includes:

- model suspension
- review of features used
- forced explainability using SHAP, LIME, or integrated techniques
- impact documentation and mitigation proposal

Another common risk is discontinuity in automatic training. In pipelines running daily or weekly, any failure can leave the system outdated. The contingency plan may include:

- alerts on retraining failure
- automatic fallback to the previous day's model
- blocking deployment if validation is missing

It is important to register execution dates as tags in MLflow to facilitate inspection:

python

```python
mlflow.set_tag("execution_date",
datetime.today().strftime("%Y-%m-%d"))
```

Additionally, storage failures must also be addressed. Losing access to the artifact bucket can compromise model or preprocessor loading. The contingency plan requires:

- artifact replication across multiple zones
- monitoring access to buckets

- local fallback or secondary network

Common Errors and Solutions

Error: "Prediction service returns 500"
Probable Cause: Corrupted model, dependency error, or missing resource.
Recommended solution: Log the last valid model and apply automatic rollback.

Error: "Performance degradation detected too late"
Probable Cause: No post-deploy metric monitoring.
Recommended solution: Implement ground truth collection and automated comparison system.

Error: "Failed to reprocess run for incident analysis"
Probable Cause: Original run's code or data not versioned.
Recommended solution: Save critical artifacts as part of the run and document source code hash.

Error: "Fairness violation"
Probable Cause: Model trained on biased data, not tested across segments.
Recommended solution: Implement mandatory segmented analysis and block deployment if disparity exceeds technical limit.

Error: "Deploy without statistical validation"
Probable Cause: Failure in the pipeline's automated test stage.
Recommended solution: Create an independent validation layer with minimum promotion criteria.

Best Practices

- Create a risk matrix with impact, likelihood, and recovery time.

- Define specific contingency plans for each identified risk.

- Automate model rollback based on real metrics.

- Log code, dataset, and environment configuration as part of every run.

- Periodically test recovery plans to ensure feasibility.

- Document all incidents with timestamp, run_id, and corrective action.

- Implement alert channels with different routes by failure type (performance, ethics, technical).

- Periodically validate inference pipelines with synthetic datasets for robustness testing.

- Simulate controlled failures to verify real recovery time (chaos engineering).

- Integrate MLflow with SRE and observability tools for unified visibility.

Strategic Summary

Risk analysis and contingency planning are not optional steps —they are technical requirements in any serious Machine Learning operation. MLflow, by structuring each execution with traceability and versioning, provides the foundation to detect, respond to, and learn from incidents. Having well-defined plans means avoiding losses, maintaining trust, accelerating fixes, and strengthening technical maturity. In critical environments, anticipating failure is just as important as building solutions.

And logging every step is what turns reaction into permanent learning. Risk is not a mistake — it's an opportunity to anticipate with real engineering.

CHAPTER 25. FINAL CHECKLIST FOR MLFLOW PROJECTS

Finalizing a Machine Learning project with safety and quality requires more than achieving a good evaluation metric. It is necessary to ensure that each step of the process has been logged, versioned, validated, and documented. MLflow, by centralizing the model lifecycle, requires an execution standard that goes beyond the code and the model itself. This chapter presents a final technical checklist, validating the main operational, functional, reproducible, and strategic aspects that every project structured in MLflow must meet before being considered complete and ready for production, auditing, reuse, or scaling.

The final checklist is composed of five main blocks:

- full traceability
- technical reproducibility
- safe operationalization
- governance and documentation
- preparation for scaling and maintenance

1. Full traceability

Every project must ensure that each execution can be traced in detail, including parameters, metrics, artifacts, code version, and data source.

- were all parameters logged with mlflow.log_param() or log_params()?

- were all relevant metrics logged with mlflow.log_metric() or log_metrics()?

- was the model logged with mlflow.log_model() and linked to a compatible flavor?

- was the source code saved as an artifact or had its hash registered as a tag?

- were the input data (training, testing, or validation dataset) versioned or stored as artifacts?

- was the execution environment (conda.yaml or Dockerfile) logged along with the model?

2. Technical reproducibility

It is essential that any technical person can repeat the original execution and obtain the same result, regardless of machine or environment.

- was mlflow run used with MLproject and defined parameters?

- is the Git commit or pipeline ID associated with the run recorded?

- are all dependent files included in the project or accessible via a versioned URI?

- can the same environment (conda.yaml) be recreated from the registered run?

- were random seeds fixed and registered as parameters?

3. Safe operationalization

The model is ready to be deployed in a production environment, with support for validation, rollback, observability, and stable performance.

- was the model registered in the MLflow Model Registry with description, stage, and comments?

- is there a functional validation test after deploy?

- is a previously validated model available for fallback?

- was the expected input payload documented and tested?

- was a stress or load test performed on the endpoint with the active model?

- are production metrics (response time, errors, volume) being collected?

4. Governance and documentation

The project can be audited, presented to stakeholders, or replicated in other contexts based on the recorded evidence.

- are the author(s) and final execution date registered as tags?

- was the purpose of the run documented with mlflow.set_tag("finalidade", "...")?

- is there a technical report saved as an artifact with metrics and model justifications?

- were limitations, assumptions, and usage conditions of the model registered?

- were fairness, segmentation, or bias analyses executed

and saved?

- are all models promoted to production linked to traceable executions?

5. Preparation for scaling and maintenance

The project is prepared for retraining, adaptation, reuse in other tasks, and expansion to multiple versions or contexts.

- are the scripts parameterized and organized for automation in pipelines?

- is the project structure compatible with execution in multiple simultaneous runs?

- are previous models archived with versioning and minimal documentation?

- is the frequency of project reexecution defined (weekly, monthly retraining, etc.)?

- does the model support extension to new data or variables?

- are there auxiliary scripts for periodic cleanup, backup, and auditing?

Minimum expected project structure:

- **MLproject** — Manifest file defining all project parameters, execution environment, and entry points for reproducible execution.

- **conda.yaml** — Fully versioned environment specification listing all dependencies required to recreate the runtime context.

- **train.py** — Main training script, modularized and integrated with MLflow logging for parameters, metrics, and artifacts.

- **evaluate.py** — Script responsible for final model validation and generation of complementary artifacts such as evaluation reports, plots, and diagnostic logs.

- **/outputs/** — Directory storing all evaluation outputs including metrics, visualizations, logs, and additional diagnostic files.

- **README.md** — Project documentation including objectives, file structure, usage instructions, and execution guidelines.

- **final_report.pdf** — Technical report capturing model performance metrics, architecture, assumptions, limitations, and deployment plan.

- **run_id (final)** — Unique identifier of the production-approved run, saved and explicitly documented as the official reference for versioning, rollback, and audit purposes.

Common Errors and Solutions

Error: "Deploy made with untrackable model"
Probable Cause: Model logged outside MLflow control or not linked to a run.
Recommended solution: Standardize deploys exclusively with models registered in the Registry with description and technical origin.

Error: "Reexecution fails due to missing dependency"

Probable Cause: conda.yaml environment was not saved or is incomplete.
Recommended solution: Use mlflow.create_conda_env() or export complete environment with conda env export.

Error: "Metrics inconsistent with previous validation"
Probable Cause: Used data not versioned or altered.
Recommended solution: Save datasets as artifact or use external versioning tool like DVC.

Error: "Model deployed without fallback"
Probable Cause: Previous version not correctly registered in the Registry.
Recommended solution: Always maintain at least one previous version validated in Staging.

Error: "Project does not run outside notebook"
Probable Cause: Scripts depend on interactive context or global variables.
Recommended solution: Encapsulate logic in scripts with interface by parameters and controlled input.

Best Practices

- Use a final run as the official project reference, with all evidence recorded.

- Keep code modularized with separation between training, evaluation, and deploy.

- Validate all files needed for reexecution with hash and register as tag.

- Automate the generation of technical reports with templates integrated into the pipeline.

- Review parameter, metric, and tag names for consistency

and clarity.

- Standardize the structure of MLflow projects in repositories with replicable layout.

- Conduct a collaborative checklist before production approval.

- Validate that all paths used are relative or based on generic URIs.

- Use experiment and model names with standardized naming by team or domain.

- Store technical documentation of each model alongside the official repository or internal knowledge platform.

Strategic Summary

The final checklist is not a formality — it's an operational safeguard. It ensures that a project delivered by one person today can be reused, revalidated, scaled, or audited by any other team member tomorrow. With MLflow as tracking infrastructure, technical responsibility for every decision becomes visible, documented, and reliable. Rigor in the final delivery turns prototypes into institutional assets. And the checklist is the tool that consolidates this transformation. Models come and go. But a well-documented, complete, and reproducible project sustains growth, protects operations, and builds a culture of excellence. In the end, what sets mature technical projects apart is not only what they deliver — it's how they deliver.

FINAL CONCLUSION

Throughout this book, we have undertaken a structured and intensive journey through the universe of MLflow, progressively, practically, and technically addressing all the fundamental and advanced elements for implementing, managing, and evolving machine learning pipelines in professional environments. Now, at the end, it is essential to consolidate the key lessons learned, clearly review the strategic contribution of each chapter, and prepare the reader to apply, expand, and sustain the knowledge acquired in a continuous and efficient manner.

We began in Chapter 1 with an overview of MLflow, clarifying its purpose as an open-source platform aimed at managing the lifecycle of machine learning models. Its four main components — Tracking, Projects, Models, and Registry — were introduced, with a focus on fluid integration between development, validation, reproducibility, and deployment. The chapter emphasized understanding MLflow's role as a technical centralization hub, promoting consistency and traceability from the first experiments to the final deploy.

In Chapter 2, we explored the fundamentals of model management, presenting practices that support traceability, versioning, and governance over ML models. We discussed the importance of logging artifacts, parameters, metrics, and environments to create an auditable experimentation timeline. Mastering these practices reinforces the ability to replicate, compare, and justify results with technical rigor.

Chapter 3 detailed the architecture and internal components of MLflow, exposing the operational logic behind the modules, their interconnections, and how they integrate into external workflows. Understanding the client-server structure, RESTful APIs, and compatibility with platforms such as Databricks and Kubernetes directly contributes to building robust, scalable, and production-ready environments.

Installation and environment configuration were addressed in Chapter 4, prioritizing a secure, efficient, and modular setup. Different execution methods — local, remote, and containerized — were detailed, always considering system variables, data persistence, and secure storage. This solid foundation is critical to avoid recurring errors and ensure development stability.

In Chapter 5, we deeply explored experiment tracking, detailing how to use mlflow.log_param, mlflow.log_metric, and how to visualize runs via the web interface and API. Proper tracking captures a structured testing history, fostering comparative analysis and technical evolution of developing models.

Chapter 6 focused on artifact and resource management, discussing strategies for organizing relevant files such as scripts, datasets, trained models, and graphs. Proper artifact management is one of the pillars of technical traceability, fundamental to ensuring that each execution is documented and accessible.

In Chapter 7, we addressed the use of MLProjects as a packaging and portability standard for experiments. Using MLproject as an organizational manifest enables consistent execution across multiple environments. This chapter reinforced practices of modularity and reproducibility in development.

Chapter 8 introduced the concept of MLflow Models, explaining serialization formats, support for multiple languages (Python, R, Java), and integration with tools such as PyFunc, TensorFlow, and H2O. It also detailed logging and deployment strategies to facilitate transition from training to production environments.

In Chapter 9, we explored the model registry as a central

structure for governance, versioning, and formal model approval. The staging, production, and archived cycles were described, along with promotion and rollback policies. This control is essential for teams operating in collaborative environments with multiple model versions.

Chapter 10 presented integration with CI/CD pipelines, emphasizing the importance of connecting MLflow with tools such as GitHub Actions, GitLab CI, Jenkins, and Azure DevOps. By inserting MLflow into automated pipelines, we ensure continuous delivery, robust testing, and systematic revalidation of models as new versions are proposed.

In Chapter 11, we addressed metric visualization and analysis using the MLflow UI and APIs. Real-time visual analysis of metrics helps identify overfitting, underfitting, and error trends, promoting a data-driven culture and quantitative support for engineering decisions.

Chapter 12 addressed feature engineering and preprocessing, connecting classical data transformation practices to traceability in MLflow. Proper serialization of preprocessing steps into complete pipelines is essential to prevent divergences between training and inference.

Chapter 13 discussed security and access control, focusing on authentication, authorization, environment isolation, and data encryption. In a multi-user and regulated environment, the chapter reinforced the need to apply Zero Trust principles and practices aligned with LGPD and GDPR.

Storage scalability was the focus of Chapter 14, which presented best practices for using remote backends like Amazon S3, Google Cloud Storage, Azure Blob, and local distributed systems like MinIO. As experiments and models grow, data architecture becomes a critical factor for performance and reliability.

In Chapter 15, integration with cloud providers was highlighted, explaining automated deployments and record persistence in multicloud environments. This chapter consolidated practices for teams adopting infrastructure as a service and intelligently scaling resources.

Chapter 16 provided a comprehensive focus on model deployment in production, covering REST servers, integration with Flask, Docker, Kubernetes, and tools like SageMaker. Technical requirements, validations, security checkpoints, and rollback strategies were discussed.

Chapter 17 addressed monitoring and post-deployment, showing how to instrument applications with Prometheus, Grafana, and logging systems to capture latency metrics, failures, resource usage, and inference drifts. This operational visibility is essential to ensure performant and secure models over time.

Chapter 18 presented real-world use cases in large environments such as banks, telecoms, healthcare, and industry. Examples with high data volumes, multiple sources, and compliance requirements were analyzed, demonstrating MLflow's flexibility in the face of complex challenges.

In Chapter 19, we covered integration with AutoML, focusing on frameworks like H2O AutoML, Google AutoML, and open-source tools like Auto-sklearn and TPOT. Interoperability with these tools accelerates prototyping and enhances model performance while maintaining full traceability via MLflow.

Chapter 20 reinforced the importance of reproducibility and auditability of experiments, presenting practices for complete versioning of code, data, configurations, and environments. These strategies are mandatory for regulated projects with strong scientific rigor.

The creation of extensions and plugins was addressed in Chapter 21, showing how to customize commands, create specific interfaces for business tasks, and integrate MLflow with proprietary internal pipelines. The ability to extend MLflow enhances its strategic value for mature organizations.

Chapter 22 explored integration with Spark and Big Data, presenting strategies for processing large data volumes, training models in distributed clusters, and efficiently tracking results. Using MLflow in Spark environments enables parallel analyses with real horizontal scalability.

Chapter 23 addressed hyperparameter optimization, demonstrating integrations with tools like Hyperopt, Optuna, and GridSearchCV, in addition to Bayesian, Random Search, and genetic algorithm strategies. Tracking optimized runs via MLflow allows for evidence-based selection of the best model.

In Chapter 24, we analyzed risks and contingency plans, focusing on mitigating operational failures, data security, and rollback strategies. Prevention was highlighted as a strategic responsibility for production models.

Chapter 25 presented a final checklist for MLflow projects, consolidating the critical points of each stage of the model lifecycle — from prototype to production — and offering a reusable structure for technical validation, governance, and project evolution.

To close this journey, I reaffirm my commitment as the author to deliver not just a technical guide, but a practical and ongoing reference resource. This book was developed to accompany your professional journey, offering a solid foundation, conceptual rigor, and real applicability in any environment where machine learning models are created, trained, deployed, and monitored with excellence.

Thank you, reader. Your time, dedication, and trust in this work are deeply appreciated. May the techniques presented here become permanent tools in your daily practice and pave the way for increasingly strategic, efficient, and transformative projects. May your journey with MLflow go beyond technical mastery, reaching a level of maturity and leadership in machine learning engineering. We move forward together, always in continuous learning.

Sincerely,
Diego Rodrigues & Team